No Greater Love

Learning from Jesus' *Agape* Love

Larry J. Mouton Jr.

Sermon To Book
www.sermontobook.com

No Greater Love / Larry J. Mouton Jr.
ISBN-13: 978-1-945793-54-7
ISBN-10: 1-945793-54-6

God be praised for inspiring Pastor Larry J. Mouton Jr. to author this most timely and relevant book on the life of Christ. Not only is this book theologically accurate and doctrinally sound, but it is also extremely practical for believers' use in patterning their daily lives after the life of Christ, who is our perfect example. I highly recommend this book for use by churches, associations, and conventions, to foster growth and spiritual development in their members.

—**Rev. Dr. Bartholomew Banks**
Pastor, St John Progressive Missionary Baptist Church, Inc.;
President, Progressive Missionary & Educational Baptist
State Convention of Florida, Inc.;
Vice President At-Large, National Baptist Convention of
American International, Inc.

No Greater Love evoked a range of emotions; I was able to read and equate myself to how Jesus was treated in parts of this book. It helped me to have a better knowledge of the Bible. I now know the meaning of *agape* love, baptism, and temptation. This book taught me how and why to pray. Most importantly, I learned who Jesus was and why he died for my sins. The workbooks at the end of each chapter challenged me to recall and recite the information read. It is an easy read for anyone who wants to learn [more about] the Bible.

—**Yvette Lewis, NAACP Hillsborough County Branch president**

This is a book that everyone should read if they are serious about their walk with the Lord. God has called Pastor Larry J. Mouton Jr. for a purpose, and that is to help you fulfill what God has intended for your life.

—**Mayor Bob Buckhorn, City of Tampa**

This fantastic work by Pastor Larry J. Mouton Jr. unashamedly focuses on the rich earthy ministry of Jesus. We live in a time when there is an intentional effort afoot to lower the volume of Jesus-centered discussions. This author provides a loud and accurate accounting of the sacrificial, redemptive path of Jesus. It is refreshing to see a book closely related to the Bible. There is a lifting of the testimony to our once crucified yet living Christ. The information is arranged in a manner that walks a seeking person as well as a seasoned Christian from the birth to the resurrection and eventual declaration of the return of our Lord. Pastor Mouton preached the gospel through ink on pages. This book is highly recommended to be read by growing disciples. It is also a resource for small group Bible study. I am proud to call this pastor a beloved friend and valuable colleague in the gospel ministry.

—**Dr. Samuel C. Tolbert, Jr.**

> **Pastor, Greater St. Mary Missionary Baptist Church, Lake Charles, LA;**
>
> **President, The National Baptist Convention of America International, Inc.**

Oftentimes, our expressions of love toward others are based on our own selfish needs. This book provides practical examples of how to love unconditionally, through the eyes of Jesus, regardless of the circumstances.

—**Evelyn Collins, retired administrator and counselor, Fort Worth Independent School District**

It is with heartfelt gratitude that I dedicate this book to my loving parents: my mother, Rena Sam, who taught me to love tenderly, and my father, Leo Sam, who instructed me to labor tenaciously.

Also, to my adorable wife and high school sweetheart, Reba Mouton, who has profoundly inspired me to share my convictions about our Lord and Savior, Jesus Christ.

And to our children, Hanna and Joshuah Mouton, whom God entrusted to our stewardship. The joy of cultivating and nurturing their lives serves as a tremendous encouragement to reach others with the liberating and glorious gospel.

Finally, to a host of family, friends, and clergy who are far too numerous to name but are certainly esteemed.

To God be the glory!

CONTENTS

No Greater Love

Dr. George Crane—a newspaper columnist and minister—tells the story of a disgruntled wife who came into his office to declare that she wanted to divorce her husband. She said, "I want to not only get rid of him, but I want to hurt him in the same fashion he hurt me."

Dr. Crane suggested this ingenious plan. He said, "Why don't you consider going home and convincing your husband how much you love him? Praise him for his decent traits. Go out of your way to be as kind, compassionate, considerate, and generous as possible. Spare no efforts to please him and to enjoy him. And after you have convinced him of your undying love and your unwillingness to live without him, then drop the bomb."

This woman pondered this idea for a moment. With revenge on her mind, a sly grin on her face, and bitterness in her heart, she exclaimed, "Beautiful!" And she went home and implemented this course of action.

After about two months, Dr. Crane thought it strange that this woman did not come back to pursue her initial request, so he called her.

"Are you ready for the divorce?" he asked. "Divorce?" she replied. "Never! After my experiment, I discovered just how much I love my husband."[1]

This woman gave unconditional love a chance—and look what it did for her! It transformed her perspective, and that in turn transformed her marriage. Now, imagine an infinite unconditional love—an infinite unconditional love that is born in the heavenly realm but comes to us as sacrificial love exercised in the earthly realm.

This is the love of Jesus.

Throughout His life, Jesus taught us that love is not inactive—love is not something passive or complacent. Rather, wherever love exists, it is expressed and acted upon. We cannot say that we love without demonstrating love. This is why John said, "...the one who does not love his brother whom he has seen, cannot love God whom he has not seen (1 John 4:20 NASB).

Jesus teaches us that love is more than just prayers or empty promises. Love is established by the consistency of our deeds. That's the kind of love we see when we consider the words, "For God so loved the world, that he gave his only begotten Son..." (John 3:16). This reveals the depth and height of God's love. God's love is impartial. God's love is unbiased. *He so loved the world.* We can see the breadth of God's love in the fact that He gave it to everyone unconditionally.

Now, when the apostle John wrote his gospel and said that God so loved the world, this was baffling to his Jewish readers. They couldn't understand how God could ever love those outside the Jewish faith. They took immense pride in their rich cultural and religious heritage. In fact, they prided themselves on their rituals and ceremonies. They considered themselves to be worthy of God's love because of their devotion to the law. But not the Gentiles. The Jews considered the Gentiles to be dogs unworthy of God's love—enemies who should be shunned because they did not know the one true and living God.

Yet John shocked them by saying God so loved the *world*. Isaiah prophesied in Isaiah 42:1 that Jesus would come to bring justice to the nations (NASB)—in other words, everyone, Jews and Gentiles alike. Paul said in Romans 1:16, "For I am not ashamed of the gospel. It is the power of God that brings salvation first to the Jew, then to the Gentile" (NIV).

No one is excluded from God's love. How could God love in such a phenomenal manner? John gave us the secret: "God is love" (1 John 4:8 NASB).

Love is who He is—His very essence and nature. God loves us all despite who we may be.

Now, that may be difficult to understand. It's difficult for us to grasp, because the human love we experience is not quite like this sacrificial love we see in Scripture.

There is a pragmatic, transactional love—the love that we experience in our encounters with one another, that is dependent on one's social class or economic status. It's an arranged kind of love.

6 · LARRY J. MOUTON JR.

There is *eros* love—a physical attraction between two people. This kind of love may or may not have substance. We understand love between romantic partners, or between husbands and wives. But many of today's romances bring heartache, and many marriages end in divorce. We understand love between siblings. They love each other, yet they often wrestle with one another. The highest form of love that you and I can muster apart from God is that of *phileo* love. *Phileo* is this brotherly type of love. It is also seen between parents and children.

When you understand love only in these contexts, however, you cannot fully grasp God's sacrificial love, which is called *agape* in the Greek. *Agape* love is a selfless love. *Agape* love is dependent upon the lover, not upon the one who is being loved. That's why God can love us in spite of us. God loves us even when we're unlovely. God loves us when others say we're unlovable. God will love us even when we're unloving. God can love the unbelieving, the obstinate, the skeptical, the doubtful, the vengeful, and the spiteful. This is because God is love (1 John 4:8 NASB).

This love can look at our mistakes and love us regardless. This was mind-boggling to the Jews. In fact, this is mind-boggling in every generation.

Some may wonder, *How could God love a vile person? How could God love an immoral person? How could He love a murderer or a prostitute? How can God love a wife beater or a child abuser? How can God love a thief or an alcoholic? How can God love an oppressor or an enslaver?* It is because God *is* love (1 John 4:8).

He doesn't just love the good. He doesn't just love the true. He doesn't just love the religious. The Bible says, "…God so loved the world" (John 3:16). And God came to reveal this love to us through His Son, Jesus the Christ.

I want to show you the *proof* and the *purpose of* God's love.

The text says, "For God so loved the world, that He gave His only begotten Son…" (John 3:16). This is the proof. This is the uncontested and unequivocal evidence of God's love: He gave His only begotten Son. God loved us in the most perfect way possible. He loves us to the greatest measure and ultimate degree. God's love for you is not dependent upon you. You can respond to it or reject it. But God loves you anyway.

God gave up His Son, the One who is dearest to His heart. He gave up His Son to the world, and He gave up His Son to the cross. Both were great sacrifices. God allowed His Son to leave the splendor and brilliance, the majesty and glory of heaven, to come down to a world that was depraved and apostate, wicked and rebellious. He came to redeem a fallen humanity.

The *purpose* of God's love is that "whosoever believeth in Him should not perish but have everlasting life" (John 3:16). God gave His Son, and this was the purpose: to save us *from* perishing and to save us *into* eternal life through Jesus Christ (John 3:17). To perish in this world is one thing, but to perish in the next dimension is another.

In this life, to *perish* means "to age or to deteriorate." It also means "to be without purpose, significance, or meaning"—in other words, meandering throughout life aimlessly. To perish in this life means to be without God. In the life to come, perishing means dying, facing judgment, being condemned, suffering separation from God, and experiencing hell. God came to save us from every type of perishing.

Not only did He come to save us from perishing, He came to give us eternal life. We have no eternal life apart from Jesus Christ.

God saves us through Jesus the Christ—He is the only Way. Jesus Himself declared in John 14:6, "I am the way, the truth and the life: no man cometh unto the Father, but by me."

We live in a world that says we can save ourselves through the combined efforts of man and society. It claims that we can change our own lives. For example, if you are illiterate, you can take classes to learn how to read and overcome your situation. Or if you're overweight, you can take weight-loss pills, go on a diet, exercise, or have surgery to help you lose weight.

But we must remember that our problem runs deeper. Our problem is sin, and the only way we can overcome sin is through the blood of Jesus the Christ. Jesus gave His own life in our stead to deliver us from the curse of the law so that we might have life. It was Jesus who allowed us to have righteousness, by way of His death, without compromising His own righteousness. It was Jesus who removed the enmity that existed between humanity and a holy God. It was Jesus who removed that which hindered us from having life. It was Jesus who gave Himself on our behalf.

He died vicariously for us. Isaiah said, "...He was wounded for our transgressions, he was bruised for our iniquities: the chastisement of our peace was upon him; and with his stripes we are healed" (Isaiah 53:5). Here is the promise: "For God sent not his Son into the world to condemn the world; but that the world through him might be saved" (John 3:17).

God doesn't have to be persuaded to love or to forgive. God is not angry with us. He didn't send His Son into the world to condemn and judge us. He sent His Son into the world so we might be forgiven and saved. This is His promise: "...whosoever believeth in Him shall not perish, but have everlasting life" (John 3:16).

"*Whosoever* means exactly that; no one is excluded from His great love. Your social class, your political affiliation, your economic status—none of that matters to God. God can take our "filthy rags" (Isaiah 64:6) and make us glorious.

John said, "Greater love has no one than this, that one lay down his life for his friends" (John 15:13 NASB). Here is what He did for us: He gave of Himself. He says if we believe we will not perish.

It's imperative to know what it means to believe. Believing is not merely embracing a historical fact. It's not just an intellectual assent, in which you grasp something that you know to be true. It's not just mental conviction. It's not just head knowledge. True believing is revealed in our actions.

We don't believe until we surrender all we are and have to the Lord Jesus Christ. We don't believe until we trust Him with our past sins. We don't believe until we trust Him with our present welfare. We don't believe until we have unshakeable, unwavering hope in Him for our future destiny.

I'm reminded of a story of a little boy who made a boat.[2] He proudly took his boat, attached a string to it, put it in a river, and let the string out slowly. As the boat bobbed up and down in the water, a burst of wind suddenly filled its sails, enabling it to sail beautifully. This little boy was impressed with what he had made. But then, to his dismay, a strong current ripped the string from his grasp.

The boat was carried away, and the little boy ran alongside the shore, trying to get his boat, hopeful that the current would somehow bring the boat back to shore. But the boat just drifted farther and farther into the distance.

The little boy went home discouraged. But one day after coming home from school, he saw a boat that resembled his in a store window. He went in, looked at the boat, and saw his own initials on the bottom of it. He told the proprietor, "This is my boat." But the proprietor said to him, "I'm sorry. Somebody else brought this boat in here. If you want this boat, you're gonna have to pay for it. It's gonna cost you some money to buy this boat."

This little boy was sad and went home. But he did his chores and earned an allowance, and he went back to the store and bought back his own boat. As he was leaving, he said to the boat, "Now you're mine twice over. First I made you—and then I bought you!"

God created us for His glory, to express His essence. All of us by sin have fallen short of His glory (Romans

3:23 NIV). But He also redeemed us by the blood of the Lamb (1 Peter 1:18–19). There is no greater love than this.

Do you know that He loves you? God's love is the substance of life. He loves you unconditionally. God proves His love in the fact that He gave His Son (Romans 5:8). His purpose was to save us from perishing, to save us to eternal life, to save us through Jesus Christ. And He promised that He didn't come to condemn the world (John 3:17). He didn't come to judge the world. God's purpose in sending His Son to the world was so that the world might be saved (John 3:17).

How can we live in God's full love? How can we show that full love to a hungry world? Through the example of Jesus.

In the following pages, we will examine the life of Jesus to learn how to live and love like He did. At the end of each chapter, several workbook questions will take you deeper into these truths and give you focused applications for your life. On this journey, you'll learn how His birth, His life, His ministry, His death, and His resurrection provide the perfect example of how to live and how to love others with an *agape* love.

CHAPTER ONE

The Early Years of Christ

Now the birth of Jesus Christ was on this wise: When as his mother Mary was espoused to Joseph, before they came together, she was found with child of the Holy Ghost. Then Joseph her husband, being a just man, and not willing to make her a public example, was minded to put her away privily.

But while he thought on these things, behold, the angel of the Lord appeared unto him in a dream, saying, Joseph, thou son of David, fear not to take unto thee Mary thy wife: for that which is conceived in her is of the Holy Ghost. And she shall bring forth a son, and thou shalt call his name JESUS: for he shall save his people from their sins. Now all this was done, that it might be fulfilled which was spoken of the Lord by the prophet, saying, Behold, a virgin shall be with child, and shall bring forth a son, and they shall call his name Emmanuel, which being interpreted is, God with us.

Then Joseph being raised from sleep did as the angel of the Lord had bidden him, and took unto him his wife: And knew her not till she had brought forth her firstborn son: and he called his name JESUS.

—Matthew 1:18–25

A little boy once inquired of his mother, "Mom, how did you come here? And how did I come here?" His mother shared with him a fantastical story of how they came to earth, a tall tale of a beautiful white-feathered bird. Later, this young boy asked his grandmother, "Grandma, how did *you* come here?" She responded with a variation of the same bird story. The boy was with his friends one day soon afterward, and he said to them, "There hasn't been a normal birth in my family for three generations!"[3]

Scripture makes it abundantly clear that Jesus Christ was conceived by the Holy Spirit. A person must express his or her faith in the God of love—the God who came to save people from their sins. The God who journeyed through the umbilical cord of time to come to a fallen world—to be with us. The God who promised a Savior to His people, and then brought Him forth at just the right time.

The world longed for this Christ. The people of that time were feverishly panting for the long-awaited, promised Messiah. The weight of life was cruel. People were overwhelmed and burdened. They knew God could not wait much longer before He brought to fruition that which He had promised. The conditions of life in that day made them cry out for a Savior.

That's the time when Jesus showed up on the scene. And when your own life becomes upsetting, disrupted, or even desperate, you need to remember that He knows how to show up!

The Birth of Christ

The birth of Jesus Christ is one of the most phenomenal events in human history. However, it was disturbing to many.

What was so disturbing about the arrival of our Savior? First, there was Mary and her pregnancy. Who would believe her story, that her pregnancy was conceived by the Holy Spirit? This required her willingness to be available to God in absolute surrender, despite the shame and embarrassment or the opinions of family, friends, and neighbors.

Then there was this: Joseph was espoused to Mary. They were betrothed. They were legally bound as if they were married. Yet Mary was pregnant, and Joseph was torn between two things. The law required Mary to be exposed to the authorities because of the act of adultery that appeared to have been committed. In Joseph's day, anyone who committed an act of adultery was to be stoned to death. And Joseph was torn between his allegiance to the law and his love for his espoused. The Bible says he did not want to make her a public example. He didn't want to bring her before the authorities to be stoned. But he did want to put her away quietly. He struggled with the dilemma. He was torn between the law and his love for this woman.

Then there was the child, Jesus Himself, who was born in a smelly manger, a feeding trough. Our Savior left the glories of heaven, in all its majesty, to arrive in this world and be placed in a feeding trough?

Then as a family, they were suddenly uprooted and sent by God to a foreign nation—Egypt. This required a willingness to obey at any cost.

Then Herod commanded the slaughter of every male under two years old in Bethlehem and the surrounding areas. Joseph and Mary must have felt a great weight of responsibility when they realized that, by some measure, this incident was occurring because of their young son.

There were the wise men who journeyed from afar, and who gathered around the child Jesus to offer gifts of gold, frankincense, and myrrh to this prophet, priest, and king.

A Revelation

Look at this verse: "But while [Joseph] thought on these things, behold, an angel of the LORD appeared unto him in a dream, saying, Joseph, thou son of David, fear not to take unto thee Mary thy wife: for that which is conceived in her is of the Holy Ghost" (Matthew 1:20).

Watch what happened: Joseph was torn, and he went to God. He thought on these things. But more specifically, he prayed to God.

Joseph went to God because of his predicament, and he received a revelation. The angel of the LORD appeared to him and said, "Joseph, thou son of David" (Matthew 1:20). Every Jew knew that Jesus the Messiah would come through the Davidic line. Joseph knew that Jesus would come through the Davidic line. God revealed to Joseph that Mary's pregnancy was what was promised. It was what was prophesied. Now it was coming to fruition. In this revelation, Joseph went from being torn to being humbled, because God was using him to do something glorious.

Prophecy Fulfilled

Isaiah said, "For unto us a child is born, unto us a son is given..." (Isaiah 9:6). God enveloped Himself in human flesh and came to us. He came to offer Himself on behalf of humanity, which was guilty of violating God's law.

Jesus was prophecy fulfilled in that the Savior was to be born to a virgin (Isaiah 7:14). Additionally, it was prophecy fulfilled in the fact that His name was Emmanuel—God with us (Isaiah 7:14). This was important to the Jews because they understood the Old Testament prophecy.

Most of us think Jesus only suffered on the cross. But Jesus suffered every day of His life. He was born of a virgin. He was born in a smelly manger. He was born in despicable conditions. He was born to humble, poor parents. Even as a baby, His very life was threatened. He knew what it was like to be without a home. He moved from place to place for protection, even in childhood.

He was reared in an insignificant city called Nazareth. He didn't have a place to lay His head as an adult. He was hated and opposed and rejected by the religionist. He was constantly confronted with their hostility. He was hated by His own audience. He was rejected by His own family. At the end of His life, His closest friends left Him alone. He was forsaken and abandoned. And then, He was brought before a high court and charged with treason.

He was sentenced to the worst possible punishment—crucifixion. The Bible says, "But he was wounded for our transgressions, he was bruised for our iniquities: the chastisement of our peace was upon him; and with his stripes we are healed" (Isaiah 53:5). He came to give us life. He loved with sacrificial love and continues to love us unconditionally. He came to give us peace. Paul wrote, "Therefore being justified by faith, we have peace with God through our Lord Jesus Christ" (Romans 5:1). The redemptive work of Jesus Christ and our expressed faith in Him gives us peace with God. He came to give us hope. This hope is a confident expectation that God is able—and willing—to intercede on our behalf regardless of our situation.

Because of the birth of Christ, a fundamental change can now take place in our inward being that corresponds to our new nature. Because of His birth, we can have life and have it more abundantly.

Not only was He born and ultimately crucified, but the Bible says that on the third day, He was resurrected by God's power (2 Corinthians 13:4 NIV). There is now power to deliver us. Power to save us. Power to change us. Power to spiritually transform us. Power to give us new life. Power to give us eternal life!

Seek and Obey God

God has a purpose for your predicament, just as He had a purpose for Mary and Joseph's dilemmas. Mary and Joseph had to endure many difficult circumstances to bring Jesus into this world. We, too, must surrender to God and obey Him at any cost. Joseph teaches us that our love takes precedence over the law. The rule is never more important than the relationship. The whole purpose of the rule is to keep the relationship.

Just like the birth of Christ created a predicament for Joseph, it creates a predicament for you and me when it comes to Christ and His claims in a world filled with erroneous doctrines.

Will we be a people with the boldness and audacity to stand up and be who we are in a world that's filled with moral degradation? Or will we be a people who only do what is expected of us?

Will we be a people who praise God in church but look just like the world after we cross the threshold and leave God's house? Or will we stand strong and let love take precedence in our lives?

Stand for Jesus Christ, because only what you do for Him is going to last. You're going to be persecuted for standing up for Christ, but He says, "Blessed are they who are persecuted for my name and for righteousness' sake..." (Matthew 5:10–11). Even though you may feel overwhelmed, ashamed, and embarrassed by people who criticize you, you will have joy to sustain you on your journey with God.

Jesus's birth was unusual. No one had ever been conceived by the Holy Spirit before. Yet this is the point in the gospel where we either accept it by faith or we reject it with doubt and skepticism.

Like Joseph learned in his predicament regarding Mary's pregnancy and the birth of the Messiah into his own family, whenever we are in trouble, the best thing to do is pray to God. I'm not saying that you shouldn't seek wise counsel from other people. But your first response should be to go to God in prayer.

God revealed to Joseph what His purpose was. He helped him to understand the situation. God will always make known His purpose for our predicament when we pray to Him and trust Him for guidance. He did that for Joseph. He made it abundantly clear to Joseph the destiny of this Savior, Jesus the Christ. God gave His Son to save us from our sin, and He now calls us to participate with Him in His plans. How glorious is it that God would call us to be part of the phenomenal work He is doing in this world?

The good news is that He equips us for the task at hand and enables us to grow as we seek Him and His purpose and destiny in our own lives.

Jesus Grew

And the child grew. And waxed strong in spirit, filled with wisdom and the grace of God was upon Him.
—Luke 2:40

And Jesus increased in wisdom and stature and in favor with God and man.
—Luke 2:52

Jesus is both divine and human. When I speak of Jesus "growing," I'm not speaking in terms of perfection or maturity. In His divinity, He has natural and moral attributes, like omniscience, omnipotence, and omnipresence. He is filled with holiness, righteousness, justice, loving-kindness, and mercy.

He is all these things in His divine nature. But in His human nature, His childhood progressed in a normal way. As He grew up, He came into a broader knowledge of His calling on the earth and a clearer self-consciousness. However, there was no sinful element mingled with His growth.

In His humanness, He developed, like us. He was instructed by His parents in the Word of God. He was taught in the synagogue. He studied the writings of learned men. He communed with God in order to set an example for us. Jesus endured the limitations that you and I know, and yet He was without sin. That means that He has the power to bring forth righteousness in us. He chose to subject Himself to God the Father in such a way as to model for us what it looks like to grow up and overcome our sin nature.

Examples of Jesus' Growth

Jesus sets this example for us. As we consider His example, let us be inspired toward continual growth.

Jesus was a carpenter as a boy. Jesus labored. He prepared Himself early. As an adult, Jesus performed tasks in His mission on this earth in such a manner that it gave evidence of growth in His physical capabilities.

Jesus grew in His study of Scripture, and He learned from those who were scholars. Scripture gives evidence that Jesus grew naturally, just like you and me.

People loved being around Jesus. Certainly, there were those who ridiculed, hated, and opposed Him. But the people who *really* knew Jesus loved Him. The ones who hated Him were those against whom He testified about their evil deeds. Truly righteous people loved being in the presence of Jesus. He was invited to social gatherings. In His presence, people were joyous. People understood victory. People knew peace and love.

He was able to be in any company, with any type of person. He even ate with sinners. He didn't participate in their sin, but He wasn't a respecter of persons (Acts 10:34). He never compromised His convictions to bring redemption.

In His human nature, He grew in favor with God. The reason Jesus experienced the victory He did in His life was because of His fellowship with God. His public life was rooted in His private and personal communion with God. He communed with the Father in prayer. Jesus studied the Scripture. He was always seeking to do the will of the Father (John 4:34; John 5:30; John 6:38).

Follow His Example

The Bible says that "your body is a temple of the Holy Spirit who is in you, whom you have from God" (1 Corinthians 6:19 NASB). Our body is the dwelling place of God's Spirit. Further, having a healthy body is useful for God's work and our labor in His kingdom.

God has given us the gift of intellect, and He admonishes us to grow in wisdom. If we really understood that, we wouldn't take our academic journeys lightly. Whatever wisdom you gain from the Word of God—and others who are cultivating you, nurturing you, imparting wisdom to you, and investing in your life—you can use for the glory of God. He wants us to grow in wisdom, not so we can be sophisticated and look down on others, but so we can bless others.

If we, as believers in Jesus Christ, cultivate and nurture the art of a happy and healthy social life, we will bring joy to others. And we will make way for other people to respect our Christian principles.

We have an innate longing to belong because we were created to be in community. But it's a tragedy when you try to become everything to everybody and ultimately compromise who you are. To grow socially means we're able to reach out to people in a loving way without in any fashion compromising our convictions in Christ. We can be merciful without compromising who we are. If you're not careful, however, your pursuit of popularity can cause you to lose something in the process. You should never live your life to please people. Live your life to please God. If you please God, then other people can be blessed by you.

If you are going to have the joy that God promised in your life, then you must spend time with Him in prayer and in the Word of God. You must spend time meditating upon His truth.

Then you must obey. Whenever you do what God says to do, it brings Him glory and honor and it brings you unspeakable joy. That's what will sustain you. That's what will give you the audacity to rejoice in God, even in difficult situations. You aren't ignorant; you're just acquainted with the goodness of God. That's why you can rejoice in your difficulties.

When you commune with God, He will take your fragmented pieces and make you whole again.

If Jesus grew, we should be willing to grow as well. If we grow, we can make a difference in this world. If we grow, we will share the gospel that changes hearts and changes lives. Regardless of your history, God is able to do "exceeding abundantly above all that we ask or think, according to the power that worketh in us..." (Ephesians 3:20).

Jesus grew. He set a phenomenal example for us. He grew physically, mentally, socially, and spiritually.

The greatest thing you can do is surrender your life to Christ. The closer we get to the heart of God, the more we will grow in the Lord and increase in the knowledge and grace of God. The more our hearts reflect His heart, the more concerned we will become about the things of God as opposed to the things of this world. We will become more concerned about the less fortunate, disadvantaged, underprivileged, and disenfranchised. We won't pass by people who are broken. The closer to God we are, the more concerned we will be about one another.

This is the example Jesus set for us. He lived His life in communion with the Father, and He grew. We must devote our lives to following in His steps.

WORKBOOK

Chapter One Questions

Question: What were some of the "predicaments" created by Christ's birth and the surrounding events? What are some ways that Jesus suffered throughout His life? How is He able to relate to suffering that you have experienced or are experiencing?

_____

_____

_____

_____

_____

_____

_____

_____

_____

_____

Question: In what ways did Jesus grow? What does this teach us about His humanity and His divinity? How does His example teach us to be concerned for others?

_____

_____

_____

_____

_____

_____

_____

_____

_____

Action: Which area of growth is the most challenging for you—physical, mental, social, or spiritual? What is a goal that you can set for measurable growth in that area?

Chapter One Notes

_____

_____

_____

_____

_____

_____

_____

_____

_____

_____

_____

_____

_____

_____

_____

_____

_____

_____

_____

_____

_____

CHAPTER TWO

Jesus Was Baptized

In those days came John the Baptist, preaching in the wilderness of Judaea, And saying, Repent ye: for the kingdom of heaven is at hand. For this is he that was spoken of by the prophet Esaias, saying, The voice of one crying in the wilderness, Prepare ye the way of the Lord, make his paths straight. And the same John had his raiment of camel's hair, and a leathern girdle about his loins; and his meat was locusts and wild honey. Then went out to him Jerusalem, and all Judaea, and all the region round about Jordan, And were baptized of him in Jordan, confessing their sins.

But when he saw many of the Pharisees and Sadducees come to his baptism, he said unto them, O generation of vipers, who hath warned you to flee from the wrath to come? Bring forth therefore fruits meet for repentance: And think not to say within yourselves, We have Abraham to our father: for I say unto you, that God is able of these stones to raise up children unto Abraham. And now also the axe is laid unto the root of the trees: therefore every tree which bringeth not forth good fruit is hewn down, and cast into the fire. I indeed baptize you with water unto repentance: but he that cometh after me is mightier than I, whose shoes I am not worthy to bear: he shall baptize you with the Holy Ghost, and with fire: Whose fan is in his hand, and he will thoroughly purge his floor, and

gather his wheat into the garner; but he will burn up the
chaff with unquenchable fire.

Then cometh Jesus from Galilee to Jordan unto John, to be
baptized of him. But John forbad him, saying, I have need
to be baptized of thee, and comest thou to me? And Jesus
answering said unto him, Suffer it to be so now: for thus it
becometh us to fulfil all righteousness. Then he suffered
him. And Jesus, when he was baptized, went up straight-
way out of the water: and, lo, the heavens were opened
unto him, and he saw the Spirit of God descending like a
dove, and lighting upon him: And lo a voice from heaven,
saying, This is my beloved Son, in whom I am well pleased.
—Matthew 3:1–17

What do the golden arches of McDonald's, the dog
tags of a veteran just home from an overseas deploy-
ment, the mascot for our favorite sports team, and even
our American flag have in common? Each of these (typically) beloved items is a symbol. In and of themselves,
they are not really what is loved. It is the serviceman or
woman, the sports team—win or lose, the country in
which we were born or to which we emigrated, or even
those delicious French fries that really tug at our heart-
strings.

In the same way, a person can be married whether
they are wearing a wedding ring or not. The ring is a
symbol of a covenant relationship; it is not the relationship itself. In the same sense, we can be saved even
though we are not baptized. Like the ring, baptism is
symbolic of a covenant relationship.

And yet, despite this truth, a wedding ring *is* more
than an ordinary piece of jewelry. It represents something greater than itself. It represents a holy estate. It

represents the sacred union that exists between a husband and a wife.

I use this example because in our covenant relationship with the Lord, it is as if we are married to God. The Bible teaches that the Church is the bride of Christ, and Christ is the Bridegroom (John 3:29; Revelation 19:7; Revelation 21:2). We are in a covenant relationship with Him. And when we are baptized, it is a beautiful, symbolic act that serves as a public declaration of a private change that has occurred in our lives.

The Significance of Baptism

Let us take a look at this symbol of baptism and its significance for you and me as believers in Jesus Christ.

Some have placed a saving value on baptism, which is unwarranted by Scripture; others have changed the form of baptism for their own convenience. Still others have eliminated the essence of baptism's meaning entirely. Tragically, if we're not careful, we can begin to approach baptism as a mere rite, a mere ritual that we perform in the Church that carries no true significance.

This should never be the case, because baptism is significant! Let us glean what Jesus has made known to us in committing Himself to this baptism by His own cousin John the Baptist.

John's Call to Baptism

The Jews were familiar with a certain type of baptism. In fact, they would often baptize proselytes—converts or newcomers—into the faith. But John introduced a new element to baptism. His was a baptism of repentance. The word *repentance* means a "change of mind," and it indicates more than a mere turning away from sin. It's a change of mind that results in a change of action, a change of behavior. If we truly repent, we will change from what we used to do.

John had a warning for the Pharisees and Sadducees who flocked to him. He doubted their sincerity. John was not interested in a hypocritical life. He was interested in the kind of life that would demonstrate compassion and love in daily relationships.

John was sent to call people to repentance and to prepare the way for the coming of the Lamb of God, the One who came to take away the sin of the world. John understood his role. He understood his responsibility. Never did he go beyond it. Nor did he usurp the dignity or the prestige that belonged only to the Savior. In fact, when John's devotees begin to leave him to follow Jesus, John stated in John 3:30, "[Jesus] must increase, but I must decrease."

Further, he insisted that Jesus would be One to baptize with a greater baptism. He would baptize with the Holy Ghost and with fire (Matthew 3:11). John in no way, form, or fashion was minimizing his own work. But he was saying that where he had limitations, Jesus possessed the perfect insight and knowledge to be able to judge fairly and evaluate properly.

Jesus' Baptism

There is a beautiful picture to be found in the relationship between Jesus and John. John was the son of Zacharias and Elizabeth—Jesus's own "genetic" cousin through His mother, Mary. They had a unique relationship even when they were in their mothers' wombs. Now, here they were on the banks of the Jordan River. Jesus had journeyed from Jerusalem to where John was and asked John to baptize Him.

John, at first, was reluctant. He recognized the spiritual superiority of Christ. He declared to Jesus, "I need to be baptized by you, and do you come to me?" (Matthew 3:14 NIV). John was wise, almost before his time. The theological questions that would arise from this incident did not occur at the Jordan River at that time.

Paul later brought clarity to the significance of baptism. He said that baptism is a symbol of the death, burial, and resurrection of Jesus Christ (Colossians 2:12). It is the symbol of a believer's putting their sin to death and burying it, and when that believer is physically raised up from the water, they have symbolically been made new in Christ (Romans 6:4). Baptism identifies with the death, burial, and resurrection of Jesus Christ.

The word *baptism* comes from the Greek word *baptizo*, which means "to submerge."[4] When we go down into the water, it means that we die. We go down into the water, and our old life of sin is put to death and buried there. Then we are raised again, up out of the water, into newness of life. That means we are no longer who we

used to be—we continually progress from faith to faith
and from glory to glory (2 Corinthians 3:18).

Now, I have a question. Why was *Jesus* baptized? He
was not a sinner in need of repentance. The answer is
that Jesus was identifying with John in the baptism of
repentance. In other words, He was dedicating Himself
to the ministry of John. Jesus was baptized in order to
put His stamp of approval on a good act. Jesus was getting ready to enter an arena of proclamation and service
to God. Jesus would also take people from where they
were spiritually and lead them to the place where He
wanted them to be.

Jesus made this dedication by identification. And the
Bible says that His act was pleasing to God (Matthew
3:17). He dedicated Himself by baptism to prepare for
the work that was before Him. He allowed Himself to be
baptized because it would be the fulfillment of all righteousness.

God Was Pleased

My last point here is that God approved of this act in
order to demonstrate its significance. God spoke at Jesus' baptism and said these words, "This is my beloved
Son, in whom I am well pleased" (Matthew 3:17). The
Bible says that the heavens were open (Matthew 3:16).
The Bible says that John saw it (John 1:32). This was
unequivocal proof that God was pleased with the act. It
benefited Jesus. But it also was a benefit to John.

Baptism for Believers

John's work shows that baptism is more than just a ritual. First, we must repent. The enemy tries to compel you to keep playing with your sin. But if you keep playing with sin, you will keep flirting with the enemy, and you will become all the more entangled.

But thanks be to God for the grace that He shows us and for giving us His Son, Jesus the Christ. When we repent and turn away from sin, He takes off everything that enslaves and entangles us, that seeks to destroy us. He says then that we must come unto Him and be baptized.

It's not that baptism saves us. But it does contain a great message. It shows to the world our private declaration to God that we will follow Him, come what may. Our baptism shows everyone around us that we are committed to follow Him. When we come forth publicly and demonstrate our conviction by undergoing baptism, we are saying to the world, "For Christ I live and for Christ I will die."

If Jesus was baptized, it must also be significant for you and me as believers in Jesus Christ.

At conversion, we are indwelt with the Holy Spirit as believers in Jesus Christ. That means that He takes up residence in our hearts. That means that He dwells within us. But there is also a continuous action—a perpetual filling. To be filled means that He's guiding us. It's not a second experience; it's a continuous action. And you cannot be filled by Him if you haven't first been indwelt by Him. You can't be led by what you do not possess.

Jesus was baptized to show us the way in both water baptism and the filling of the Holy Spirit. And Jesus thought that baptism was important enough to incorporate it into His commission to the disciples to go out and evangelize the world. If Jesus did all of that, then we need to understand how important it is. It's a part of God's redemptive plan, so let's give it the important place it deserves in our own lives and ministries.

WORKBOOK

Chapter Two Questions

Question: Why did Jesus, who was sinless and had no need for redemption, choose to be baptized?

_____

_____

_____

_____

_____

_____

_____

_____

_____

_____

Question: What is the meaning and significance of baptism for the believer?

_____

_____

_____

_____

_____

_____

_____

_____

_____

_____

_____

Action: Research your own church's requirements and procedures for baptism. If you have never been baptized, discuss with your pastor when and how you can take this important step in your Christian life.

Chapter Two Notes

CHAPTER THREE

Jesus Overcame Temptation

And Jesus being full of the Holy Ghost returned from Jordan, and was led by the Spirit into the wilderness, Being forty days tempted of the devil. And in those days he did eat nothing: and when they were ended, he afterward hungered. And the devil said unto him, If thou be the Son of God, command this stone that it be made bread.

And Jesus answered him, saying, It is written, That man shall not live by bread alone, but by every word of God. And the devil, taking him up into an high mountain, shewed unto him all the kingdoms of the world in a moment of time.

And the devil said unto him, All this power will I give thee, and the glory of them: for that is delivered unto me; and to whomsoever I will I give it. If thou therefore wilt worship me, all shall be thine.

And Jesus answered and said unto him, Get thee behind me, Satan: for it is written, Thou shalt worship the Lord thy God, and him only shalt thou serve.

And he brought him to Jerusalem, and set him on a pinnacle of the temple, and said unto him, If thou be the Son of God, cast thyself down from hence: For it is written, He shall give his angels charge over thee, to keep thee: And in their hands they shall bear thee up, lest at any time thou dash thy foot against a stone.

And Jesus answering said unto him, It is said, Thou shalt not tempt the Lord thy God. And when the devil had ended all the temptation, he departed from him for a season.
—Luke 4:1-13

How do you prepare for a new job or a big new project at work?

In many cases, maybe you'd simply buy some new clothes, eat a good dinner, and get some extra sleep. Other times, you might also need to sign up for special training beforehand or attend an orientation to fully prepare you for your new undertaking.

Jesus was about to begin His life's work, and He needed to hear the voice of God and set His ambitions in perfect harmony with the purposes the Father had designed for Him. But right after His baptism, Jesus was confronted by the devil in a wilderness experience that showcased three different temptations. This was to reinforce and strengthen Jesus in preparation for what was to come.

Jesus successfully overcame each temptation. He models for us what we must surrender so that we might overcome the temptations we will inevitably confront. God gives us the means to overcome these temptations through His grace.

Temptation of the Flesh

Verses 3 says, "And the devil said unto him, If thou be the Son of God, command this stone that it be made bread" (Luke 4:3–5). Satan attempted to convince Jesus to use His divine power and ability in an illegitimate way.

Jesus demonstrated that God's favor and grace are not meant to be used for our own purposes. Jesus was hungry. He had been without food for forty days and forty nights. Jesus *could* have turned the stones into bread. He certainly had the power to do so. But He did not, because He did not want to demonstrate an allegiance to Satan.

Instead He said, "Man shall not live by bread alone, but by every word of God" (Luke 4:4).

Temptation of the Eye

The devil told Jesus, "All this power will I give thee, and the glory of them: for that is delivered unto me; and to whomsoever I will I give it. If thou therefore wilt worship me, all shall be thine." (Luke 4:6–7).

With these words, the enemy tried to get our Savior to compromise His ambition. Jesus' purpose was to secure the loyalty of man to God and to establish the eternal kingdom of God forever. But the enemy showed Him other kingdoms.

The enemy tried to entice Him by showing Him all these kingdoms in enormous glory. The devil was essentially saying, "Listen, I have influence and control over their possessions and their glory and I will give You all of these things if You worship me" (see Luke 4:6–7). Satan claimed that he had ownership of what actually belonged to the Lord.

Elsewhere Jesus actually substantiated the devil's claim. Jesus said that Satan is the prince of this world (John 14:30). The apostle Paul wrote that Satan is the "prince of the power of the air, the spirit that now worketh in the children of disobedience" (Ephesians 2:2) And in 2 Corinthians 4:4, he referred to Satan as the "god of this world."

If Jesus had compromised His ambition, He would have had to compromise His standards, His behavior, His mission, and ultimately, His allegiance to God. Jesus was not going to compromise anything. He only did what the Father commanded.

Temptation of Pride

Luke 4:9 describes the third temptation of Jesus: "And he brought him to Jerusalem, and set him on a pinnacle of the temple, and said unto him, If thou be the Son of God, cast thyself down from hence."

All throughout this discourse, Jesus had reminded Satan of the Word of God. But then Satan got tricky and started trying to use Scripture for his own benefit.

Satan said, "For it is written, He shall give his angels charge over thee, to keep thee" (Luke 4:10). He said, in essence, "You can be a sensation to the people because of what Scripture says." Did you catch that? Jesus was tempted to be a sensation to the people—because of what Scripture said.

Now, we might think that Jesus would be completely willing to do what is written about in the Word of God. And the truth is, God would have done whatever it took to take care of His Son. However, Jesus knew that such an action would have been inconsistent with His required obedience to God, and it would only have been a "sensation" for the people—not of any real benefit.

Satan tried to deceive Jesus into thinking that the people would be so amazed by such a feat that they would believe in Him and His mission. But Jesus was unwilling to take the bait. You see, He knew that the crowd would try to force Him to meet their own expectations and place an earthly crown on His head. But Jesus knew up front that the shortcut of "favor with men" wasn't worth it, because it would never yield God's long-term approval.

It is wise to do what Jesus did. Whenever Jesus was confronted with a crisis, He went to a place of solitude for prayer and meditation. It was necessary for Him to commune with His Father. It was essential for Him to meditate. His example teaches us how we should respond when we are faced with temptation.

Temptation: A Test

Sometimes God allows us to be confronted by temptation for the sake of awakening us. That might seem strange, because when we think about temptation, we tend to believe that we are being seduced into sin, that we are being pulled into sin. But when you consider the word *temptation* in light of its meaning in the Greek language, you understand that it also has another meaning: God can use temptations to try us—that is, to prove us, perfect us, reinforce us, and strengthen us.

We understand that teachers give lectures to their students. But they also administer tests to measure what their students have learned. They do this to develop their skills—to build them up, not destroy them.

In much the same way, God will use tests, or temptations, to awaken us. Sometimes God will allow just a little temptation to help make us strong. If we're not strong enough to stand against temptation, we will fold and collapse. It's imperative to understand that God allows this to strengthen us, to reinforce us. And He never gives us more than we are able to handle.

Dependency on God

Jesus wanted to do *all* of His ministry God's way. If He had turned the stone into bread, He would have demonstrated a trust in only Himself and a failure to rely and depend exclusively upon the will of the Father.

He would have been operating completely independent of God, and He would have been setting an example for you and me that we can use our gifts for selfish reasons, to the disregard of the less fortunate, disadvantaged, and underprivileged of this world.

Instead, His refusal demonstrated that we are not to use our abilities to build ourselves up with pride. He shows it's not about us; it is about God and His glory.

We all have physical needs—food, shelter, clothing. We also have needs for work, rest, and relationship. But

God says that's not all we need. We will never realize the quality of life that God longs for us to have if we are living by "bread" alone. We need the things that are spiritual.

Too many people are trying to be everywhere and everything to everybody. But you can only be who God created you to be. Do what you can with where you are and what you have been given, and do it to the glory of God.

The temptation of the eye may look good, but the other side of the fence only has green grass until you get there and realize it's just turf. The truth is, if we cultivate and nurture and fertilize what God has given us, we don't need to stray from His will to foster true green in our lives.

Don't let what looks good to you but is outside of His will deceive you into thinking that it's good for you.

Trusting in the Lord

Jesus said, "Thou shalt not tempt the Lord thy God" (Luke 4:12). In other words, we should not do something foolish just to provoke God to perform a miracle on our behalf.

We may be confronted with temptation, but we must use the wisdom of God to obey His Word and conform our lives to His will. Don't let Satan convince you to twist the Word to suit your own purposes. Temptation may look good to us, and it may sound appealing, but we must do what the Lord says.

The next time you are confronted with the temptation to give up and walk away, I encourage you not to quit. Don't throw in the towel. Don't walk away. Don't stop progressing. Believe that God is able to do what He has promised.

He sent His Son, Jesus the Christ, to emancipate us. He came to empower us to overcome that which enslaves us. We don't have to stumble over temptation. If we trust God, He will enable us to be victorious.

God has gifted you. God has called you with a purpose for His glory. Follow Jesus' example: Do not allow temptations to knock you down and keep you from fulfilling what God intended for your life!

WORKBOOK

Chapter Three Questions

Question: In what ways did Satan tempt Jesus, and how did Jesus respond?

_____

_____

_____

_____

_____

_____

_____

_____

_____

_____

_____

Question: What is one reason God sometimes allows us to be tempted?

_____

_____

_____

_____

_____

_____

_____

_____

_____

_____

Action: What are the greatest temptations that you face in each of these areas—the flesh, the eyes, and the pride of life? Write out and memorize specific Scriptures to help you defend against each temptation in the future.

Chapter Three Notes

_____

_____

_____

_____

_____

_____

_____

_____

_____

_____

_____

_____

_____

_____

_____

_____

_____

_____

_____

CHAPTER FOUR

Jesus Called People to Change the World

And Jesus, walking by the sea of Galilee, saw two brethren, Simon called Peter, and Andrew his brother, casting a net into the sea: for they were fishers. And he saith unto them, Follow me, and I will make you fishers of men. And they straightway left their nets, and followed him. And going on from thence, he saw other two brethren, James the son of Zebedee, and John his brother, in a ship with Zebedee their father, mending their nets; and he called them. And they immediately left the ship and their father, and followed him.

And Jesus went about all Galilee, teaching in their synagogues, and preaching the gospel of the kingdom, and healing all manner of sickness and all manner of disease among the people. And his fame went throughout all Syria: and they brought unto him all sick people that were taken with divers diseases and torments, and those which were possessed with devils, and those which were lunatick, and those that had the palsy; and he healed them. And there followed him great multitudes of people from Galilee, and from Decapolis, and from Jerusalem, and from Judaea, and from beyond Jordan.

—Matthew 4:18–25

Jesus' disciples had issues.

Peter spoke too quickly; he was impetuous and impulsive. Matthew was a tax collector who was hated by other Jews for tricking people out of their money. Thomas was a doubter with a gloomy, discouraged disposition. And Judas, of course, was a betrayer and had issues with embezzling and lies. Yet Jesus called them *all*!

The Call of Christ

Jesus came upon the first of those He would call to become His disciples in John 1. He began this process by calling Andrew, the first disciple, who would engage in the mission of sharing the glorious gospel until his death. Jesus called Simon, whom we know as Peter. Later He called Phillip and Bartholomew (who was also known as Nathanael).

Jesus's call here was a call to personal salvation. But He also called these men to leave their work, their profession, their industrious labor, and come follow Him.

He called His disciples unto Himself. We see that Peter came to know Jesus in a personal and intimate way. In fact, when Jesus inquired of Peter, "Whom say ye that I am?" Peter declared, "Thou art the Christ, the Son of the living God" (Matthew 16:15–16).

Nathanael also made a great confession when he reached this same conviction. He declared in John 1:49, "...thou art the Son of God; thou art the King of Israel."

What was happening here? These men were being brought to Jesus one by one. And they would form the

NO GREATER LOVE · 55

nucleus of the group that would come to be known as the twelve apostles.

Jesus was in Judea when He first called Andrew and Peter. Then, in Galilee, He called them a second time. There is no record in the Bible that demonstrates what Andrew and Peter did from the first time when Jesus called them until the second time He made His appeal. But one thing we do know: Jesus made a personal appeal and left an indelible imprint on their hearts and minds, because the second time He called, they left their nets immediately. They didn't allow what they were doing, their own plans and ambitions, to hinder them from responding to the call of Jesus.

Christ Calls Us to Receive Him

When we are called to follow Jesus Christ, we are first called to know Him personally. In the same manner that Jesus called His disciples in that day, He calls us. The first thing to which He calls us is personal salvation, to know Him in this intimate and personal way. We are not called to follow a worldview, a philosophical position, or an ideology; we are called to follow Jesus Christ Himself.

All of the disciples were called first and foremost to know Jesus personally. If we are going to effectively, faithfully, and diligently do what God has called us to, we must *know* Jesus Christ!

The more we know Jesus and the fellowship of His suffering, the more we will know Him in the resurrection of His power and the clearer life will become to us. We will not be mixed up or confused about all the stuff that's going on around us. Our focus will be on doing what God has called us to do, in the time that He has permitted us to do it.

Christ Calls Us to Ministry

After we have committed to following Christ and grown to know Him in a personal and intimate manner, He then calls us to action in His kingdom. And when Christ calls us to action, we sometimes make excuses. We talk about it being inconvenient or we simply declare ourselves inadequate. But when we love God, we will respond immediately to His call.

We should have the audacity to reach out and love others—no matter who it is that God calls us to approach. It doesn't matter how unlovable or even unreachable a person seems; we should respond to God's call without hesitation.

Some people receive the call to God's salvation and their call to service in the same moment. Some of us experience a lapse of time between our call to personal salvation and our call to service. No matter how it happens, God calls all of us. And no matter what our hangups may be, He calls us to ministry.

Christ Has a Distinct Call for You

Your call is different from my call. No matter where each of us is in life, we are different by design. We are different in personality. And when He calls us, He respects our personalities. God knows who you are because He created you to be who you are.

Some of us have lost our perspective of who we are. But God knows whom He has created. God knows whom He has called. God knows how He has gifted you. And God places you in certain situations according to what He has purposed and planned for your life.

Jesus' disciples had their share of issues, but Jesus still called them all together. And God has called us all together for His purpose despite our own hang-ups. He is calling us to be bold and to stand up for Him. He's calling us to be courageous. He is not concerned with who you used to be—no, who you are today is what matters to God.

Your life is new. You've been regenerated, you've been made whole again. You are a new creation in Christ. You're not who you used to be, and He will continue to shape you into His image every day. He will provide you with everything you need to fulfill His calling upon your life as you continue to learn from Him.

You and I may be tempted to reject His call, but He will continue to extend the invitation for us to know Him and to serve Him. Indecision is a form of refusal. Even if you remain undecided, God will persist in calling you.

The greatest discovery you will ever make in this life is the will of God for your life. And the greatest achievement you will ever have is to fulfill God's purpose and plan for your life. You can only experience the true joy that God has for you if you pursue His will.

Jesus knows who you are. He knows everything you've ever done. But He loves you enough to show you mercy and grace and to use you for His purposes. People may look at you as if you aren't enough, but God has called you for His glory.

So many people who started on the journey with Jesus left their places of business, their leisure activities, their recreational hobbies, and their institutions of learning, and they followed Jesus—in order to revolutionize the world. We will only discover who we are and understand all the graces we hope to know in life by pursuing a relationship with Jesus Christ. When we surrender to Him, He will reveal His calling on our lives and then use us to make a difference in this world.

WORKBOOK

Chapter Four Questions

Question: What does it mean that Christ called the disciples—and that He calls each of us—first and foremost to Himself?

_____

_____

_____

_____

_____

_____

_____

_____

_____

_____

Question: Each of the disciples had "issues." What issues (past or present) are you allowing to define you or to hinder you? Ask Christ to help you walk in the reality of being a new creation in Him.

_____

_____

_____

_____

_____

_____

_____

_____

_____

_____

Action: How would you define God's distinctive call on your life? Ask your pastor for a recommendation for a spiritual gifts evaluation to help discern areas of ministry into which God might be leading you.

Chapter Four Notes

_____

_____

_____

_____

_____

_____

_____

_____

_____

_____

_____

_____

_____

_____

_____

_____

_____

_____

CHAPTER FIVE

Jesus Gives New Meaning to Life

When therefore the Lord knew how the Pharisees had heard that Jesus made and baptized more disciples than John, (Though Jesus himself baptized not, but his disciples,) He left Judaea, and departed again into Galilee. And he must needs go through Samaria. Then cometh he to a city of Samaria, which is called Sychar, near to the parcel of ground that Jacob gave to his son Joseph. Now Jacob's well was there. Jesus therefore, being wearied with his journey, sat thus on the well: and it was about the sixth hour. There cometh a woman of Samaria to draw water: Jesus saith unto her, Give me to drink. (For his disciples were gone away unto the city to buy meat.) Then saith the woman of Samaria unto him, How is it that thou, being a Jew, askest drink of me, which am a woman of Samaria? for the Jews have no dealings with the Samaritans. Jesus answered and said unto her, If thou knewest the gift of God, and who it is that saith to thee, Give me to drink; thou wouldest have asked of him, and he would have given thee living water. The woman saith unto him, Sir, thou hast nothing to draw with, and the well is deep: from whence then hast thou that living water? Art thou greater than our father Jacob, which gave us the well, and drank thereof himself, and his children, and his cattle? Jesus answered and said unto her, Whosoever drinketh of this water shall thirst again: But whosoever drinketh of

the water that I shall give him shall never thirst; but the
water that I shall give him shall be in him a well of water
springing up into everlasting life.

—John 4:1–14

God loves all people, plain and simple. You may encounter people who make estimations about others and how they may (or may not!) measure up to God's standards. But God is no respecter of persons (see Acts 10:34). God does not love a person based on his or her merits. He loves them no matter who they are.

In a world that's parched and dying for the righteousness and goodness of God, it's crucial for us to respond as Jesus would to those who come seeking the water that satisfies their spiritual thirst.

Jesus' Approach

Jesus spent time in Judea and did ministry there before launching out to Galilee, where He conducted extended ministry.

But which path did Jesus take to go to Galilee? That is an important question because it helps us understand something God desires us to know. If Jesus had taken the traditional route, He would have journeyed to Jericho, crossed the Jordan River on the east side, and continued to travel north until He reached Berea, past Samaria. He then would have cut back over on the west side of the Jordan River before He got to Galilee.

That's important to understand, because the Jews had a hatred for the Samaritan people that ran so deep, they would not even pass through the region, much less associate with the people who lived there.

This animosity began long before Jesus' day. Around 722 B.C., the king of Assyria took most of Israel into captivity. The Assyrians then brought Gentiles into what had been Israel to resettle the land, and the Gentiles began to intermarry with the Jews who had been left there. Later, the southern kingdom of Judah also fell, and its inhabitants were also taken into captivity.

When a remnant of Jews was allowed to return to rebuild Jerusalem, they encountered these "Samaritans"— Jews and Gentiles who had entered into mixed marriages and blended their religious practices. The Jewish remnant despised them for this and denounced the Samaritans completely. So the Samaritans built a rival temple on Mount Gerizim, and they set themselves apart as the "true" descendants of Abraham, Isaac, and Jacob.[5]

This was the reason Jews and Samaritans hated each other.

But Jesus did something that was mind-boggling to those in His day. He said He was going to Samaria. Jesus went to Samaria because His compassion compelled Him to go to the place the Jews so thoroughly hated. He wanted His disciples to know that God loves all people.

In our text is a Samaritan woman. She clearly had deep moral issues and real personal problems. And yet, because Jesus loved this woman, He had the audacity to go to her and demonstrate that love in a way she would be able to understand.

Jesus's disciples had gone into the city to buy food, so He seized the opportunity to speak to this woman one on one. He knew her condition and her situation, and He didn't want to talk to her in the presence of everyone else in her community. That teaches us something else. When we know that people have issues, we don't need to bring in a crowd.

If you really love somebody, go to that person and speak to them in love; don't speak to them condescendingly. Jesus went to her and spoke with her one on one. He didn't talk about her story. He didn't throw her problems and shortcomings in her face. Jesus approached her tenderly and asked her for a drink of water.

Our Response to Jesus

The Samaritan woman would likely have been immediately suspicious when Jesus started talking to her, because Samaritans and Jews did not get along, nor did men approach women for a conversation in that culture or time. Naturally, she would have been reluctant to continue speaking with Him.

Her response to Him was, "How is it that thou, being a Jew, askest drink of me, which am a woman of Samaria? for the Jews have no dealings with the Samaritans" (John 4:9).

She essentially said to Jesus, "Our people don't even get along, so why would You ask me for such a thing? In fact, why are You here in the first place?" (see John 4:9).

Jesus said to her, "If thou knewest the gift of God, and who it is that saith to thee, Give me to drink; thou wouldest have asked of him, and he would have given thee living water" (John 4:10). Jesus's answer to this woman stirred her curiosity and interest.

Perhaps Jesus wanted this woman to understand the spiritual overtones in His words. But clearly, based upon her response, she missed their significance. In verses 13 and 14, He offered more spiritual implications, and still she missed their significance.

The story continues: "The woman saith unto him, Sir, give me this water, that I thirst not, neither come hither to draw. Jesus saith unto her, Go, call thy husband, and come hither" (John 4:15–16). Jesus was bringing the real issues to the surface.

Their conversation went from the need for physical water to the need for spiritual water. Jesus wanted to open her heart and mind so that she could recognize her personal need for the Messiah. We can't really experience or benefit from the promise of God's grace until we recognize that we are actually living apart from Him.

Jesus didn't bring this up to degrade her. His intention was to awaken her and make her aware of her spiritual condition. What Jesus did in His statement was to remind her that her former life and her present life were the root of her real condition. And this became a springboard from which Jesus could confront her real issues—not to condemn her, but so that she might be set free.

Jesus, the Messiah

The Samaritans considered themselves to be the descendants of Abraham, which they believed was enough to make them righteous before God. But Jesus said that true worship takes place when we surrender to God, regardless of our heritage. Before He announced His messiahship to this woman, He had to teach her about true worship.

Yet she still missed it at first. In verse 25, she said, "I know that Messiah (called Christ) is coming. When he comes, he will explain everything to us" (John 4:25 NIV).

The Messiah Himself stood in the presence of this woman, having a conversation with her, but she still didn't recognize Him. Isn't it amazing when you see people who are in God's very presence doing everything except worshiping Him? It's amazing to me that we can be in the presence of God, right where there is liberty available to us, and still miss it.

Finally, Jesus plainly identified Himself as the long-awaited Messiah, the One who had been promised. He let her know that He, the Messiah, was standing before her. He demonstrated incomprehensible love to her. And she believed.

Approach People with Love

God loves each person simply for who he or she is. This should encourage us to love one another without hang-ups, barriers, or parameters. We need to have the boldness to love other people because God loves us all.

The Bible says in 1 John 4:8 that "God is love." And if His Spirit dwells in us, it is inevitable that we will love others, because love is within us and will naturally flow out of us. We can love even our enemies. When people talk about you and criticize you, you can love them anyway—not because what they do is right, but because of who you are in Christ.

God gave His love to us even though we didn't deserve it. How dare we withhold from others what God freely gave us! Open your heart and let God's love flow out from you to others.

God's love knows no conditions. God's love knows no boundaries. God can take any person and change their heart by His divine power. That's what makes God's grace so amazing!

I've seen God's grace take a gangster and make him a deacon. God's grace can take a prostitute and make her a missionary. God's grace can take a person the world considers a nobody and make them somebody—all to bring glory to Himself.

God's grace is phenomenal and mind-boggling. I can't figure it out with my imperfect intellect. I can't figure it out with my limited knowledge. I can't figure out God's grace in my human condition. But His grace is boundless.

That's why we should always have the boldness to share God's love with anyone we encounter. That's what Jesus did for the Samaritan woman, and it's what He does for us. He demonstrates His unconditional love.

Jesus approached this woman gently. He answered her questions even when she opposed Him. Even though she did not fully appreciate His words at first, He recognized the necessity of bringing her attention to her desperate need for Him.

Whenever we approach someone to share the glorious message of God's grace, we must remember to select the best approach. Don't assess the person's faults and then belittle and degrade them for those issues or try to shove the gospel down their throat.

The next time the world asks you for a drink, kindly and gently offer them the Living Water. You may ask, "When did they ask me to give them a drink?" When they come to you with their problematic situation. When they come to you with their troubles and difficult circumstances. They're not asking for your perspective. They are crying out from a dire need for the Living Water. Be ready to give them the grace you yourself have received through Jesus Christ.

WORKBOOK

Chapter Five Questions

Question: Why did Jesus bring up the Samaritan woman's questionable past? How did this steer both the conversation and her thinking?

_____

_____

_____

_____

_____

_____

_____

_____

_____

_____

_____

Question: What can you learn from Jesus' approach to this encounter about sharing Christ with someone who is from a different culture or background than you?

_____

_____

_____

_____

_____

_____

_____

_____

_____

_____

_____

_____

Action: Join with your church or a local organization to minister to people who have a different lifestyle or culture from your own. Use principles from Jesus' conversation with the Samaritan woman to guide your interactions.

Chapter Five Notes

_____

_____

_____

_____

_____

_____

_____

_____

_____

_____

_____

_____

_____

_____

_____

_____

_____

_____

_____

_____

_____

CHAPTER SIX

Jesus Loved and Believed in People

And Jesus went about all the cities and villages, teaching in their synagogues, and preaching the gospel of the kingdom, and healing every sickness and every disease among the people. But when he saw the multitudes, he was moved with compassion on them, because they fainted, and were scattered abroad, as sheep having no shepherd. Then saith he unto his disciples, The harvest truly is plenteous, but the labourers are few; Pray ye therefore the Lord of the harvest, that he will send forth labourers into his harvest.

—Matthew 9:35–38

Maya Angelou might have put it best when she said that love knows no barriers. Love can jump over fences, leap over hurdles, penetrate through walls, and arrive at its destination full of hope.[6] When we have that kind of love and compassion, nothing is impossible for us. No life will go untouched when we demonstrate that kind of love in our world today.

We're living in a time when the world is in a state of confusion. But true compassion compels us to reach out. True compassion causes us to help show someone the way. We are called to help other people because that is exactly what Jesus did. When He saw the people of His world in confusion, it stirred His heart. Humanity's hurt is perpetually within the orbit of Christ's interest. Christ is always concerned about others—and we should be, too.

Jesus Provides Abundant Life

In the previous two chapters of the Book of Matthew, Jesus healed a leper. He healed the servant of a centurion. He healed Peter's mother-in-law. He cast out demons from people who were possessed. He was also on a boat with His disciples when a mighty storm arose. And the Bible says that Jesus woke up, rebuked the sea and wind, and a great calm fell upon the sea.

On the other side of the Jordan, Jesus healed two other possessed men. He healed a paralyzed man. He called Matthew, who was hated and detested. Yet Jesus saw good in him and had the audacity to call him to discipleship. Jesus healed a woman who had been suffering from a hemorrhage for twelve long years. He healed the daughter of a certain ruler in the city. He healed two men who were blind. He healed the mute and caused them to speak.

Jesus did all these wonderful things for the sake of helping others—emotionally, mentally, spiritually, and physically. Jesus wanted people to live out the abundant life He provides. He wanted them to live with significance.

The Bible says that when He viewed these people, His heart was touched. It says that He was "moved with compassion" when He saw the multitude in their state. As a result, He commissioned His disciples to spread His glorious gospel and help heal the hurt of humanity.

Jesus Saw Confusion

God never intended for there to be confusion in His world. When God created the heavens and earth, He created us all to walk together in harmony. It grieved Jesus to see people walking inconsistently with the way God had created them to walk. He saw them living in a state of confusion, and He knew He needed to make a change.

He was moved with compassion for them because they had fainted. They were bewildered. One reason they were confused was because many people were advocating erroneous doctrines. There were false teachers among them spreading lies. They were not teaching the truth that would lead the people to the heart of God. The Scriptures say in 2 Timothy 4:3, "For the time will come when they will not endure sound doctrine; but after their own lusts shall they heap to themselves teachers, having itching ears." This means that people will like what appeases them rather than the truth that challenges them.

The people were led astray by lies. They had grown weary. They had more interest in ceremonies and routines and bureaucracy than they did in the truth of God's

Word. They were a people who upheld the law and forgot the relationship that was behind the law.

Jesus saw these people broken and confused—as sheep having no shepherd. They were scattered and wandering. They had gone astray. They needed a real shepherd to care for them by telling them the truth.

A real shepherd will be courageous enough to lead people to the heart of God by proclaiming the truth. A real shepherd will lead you to the green pastures. A real shepherd will lead you to still waters. A real shepherd knows what real nourishment is. A real shepherd is not concerned about his own needs. A real shepherd wants you to know the heart of God. But these people were confused.

Jesus Had Compassion

True compassion is a deep inward movement toward another individual—a yearning to show mercy and empathy. It is the very seat of man's affection.

Compassion led Jesus to leave the splendor of heaven to come down and redeem fallen humanity. Compassion led Him to Calvary. Compassion enabled Him to endure all that He endured for us.

Jesus had compassion for the people. He showed this in three ways: teaching, preaching, and healing. Each of these actions is essential; they are not as effective when used independently from the others.

Jesus preached to inspire, to strengthen, to challenge, and to awaken. In fact, the Bible says in 1 Corinthians 1:18 that "the preaching of the cross is to them that perish foolishness; but unto us which are saved it is the power of God." He preached to awaken the people spiritually.

He also taught. He rooted people. He established them in the fertile soil of His grace. He then healed them to meet their physical, emotional, and mental needs.

Jesus Commissions Us

We can't save the world, but we are called to be witnesses. We're not saviors; we are believers. God has given us the power of the Holy Spirit to be witnesses for Him. Every single person who is a believer in Jesus Christ has been commissioned by Him.

As a Church, we're not called to meander along thoughtlessly. The truth is, we are called to be inspired and strengthened and challenged. And when we go beyond the walls of our own local church, we are called to share the glorious gospel.

Then saith he unto his disciples, The harvest truly is plenteous, but the labourers are few; Pray ye therefore the Lord of the harvest, that he will send forth labourers into his harvest.
—Matthew 9:37–38

Why were the laborers so few? The laborers are so few because many reject the call of God, because many postpone the call of God, and because many engage in false preaching and teaching.

Yet Jesus says that the harvest is plenteous. There are billions of people all around the globe who stand in need of the glorious gospel of Jesus Christ. He paints a picture on the canvas of our minds of fields and fields and fields of people who need to be harvested and gathered. There are people ripe for salvation, and if we do not "pick" them, Jesus says they will rot in the field. There is a harvest, and He has called us as laborers to go into the harvest and do the work. We must go.

Chapter Six Questions

Question: What causes the confusion of being "like sheep without a shepherd"? What are the characteristics of our true Shepherd?

_____

_____

_____

_____

_____

_____

_____

_____

_____

_____

Question: How would you define compassion?

_____

_____

_____

_____

_____

_____

_____

_____

_____

_____

_____

Action: "Every single person who is a believer in Jesus Christ has been commissioned by Him." How would you define your personal mission field? What steps can you take to be more intentional about ministering where God has placed you? Choose one way you can be more involved in the greater work beyond your own field, and then take steps toward that goal.

Chapter Six Notes

_____

_____

_____

_____

_____

_____

_____

_____

_____

_____

_____

_____

_____

_____

_____

_____

_____

_____

CHAPTER SEVEN

Jesus Taught the Model Prayer

After this manner therefore pray ye: Our Father which art in heaven, Hallowed be thy name. Thy kingdom come, Thy will be done in earth, as it is in heaven. Give us this day our daily bread. And forgive us our debts, as we forgive our debtors. And lead us not into temptation, but deliver us from evil: For thine is the kingdom, and the power, and the glory, for ever. Amen.

—Matthew 6:9–13

Did you know that God has called us to be a people of prayer?

It's not enough just to walk with Him and have a knowledge of Him in this world. We must commune with Him! And we do that through prayer.

For this reason, we ought to do more praying and less complaining. It's prayer that brings us to the highest and deepest spiritual life. It's prayer that makes all the difference in the world. The more we pray, the more we will understand the heart of God, the more we will long for God, the more we will hunger and thirst after Him, and the more we will pursue His righteousness and His kingdom.

How important is prayer in your life?

Pray even when you don't feel like praying. Pray without ceasing (1 Thessalonians 5:17). Pray knowing by faith that God will do that which He wills, and that He has the power to bring to fruition all that He wills.

The Lord's Prayer

Of the many instances found in the Scriptures of Jesus giving instructions to His followers, this is one of the most significant—because Jesus is teaching His disciples how to pray. Jesus didn't teach the Lord's Prayer to His followers just so people would recite the words throughout history. No, this is the basis and the premise upon which we must pray consistently. Here, we find what we ought to pray about.

Jesus begins with a doxology, a word simply meaning "to praise." We are to give praise to God to recognize His sovereignty and express our thankfulness for who He is.

Next in the model prayer, there is surrender and acknowledgment.

The Jews in Jesus' time were so fearful of approaching God that they would not even mention His name for fear of taking Him too lightly or approaching Him irreverently. We should approach God reverently as well! God's name is holy, and His name is pure. We need to recognize the sovereignty and the majesty of God.

Second in the model prayer, there is a petition and a plea. What should we be petitioning for? For God's kingdom to come, and for His will to be done. And what should we be pleading for? First, for God to "give us this day our daily bread" (Matthew 6:11). Second, for God to "forgive us our debts, as we forgive our debtors" (Matthew 6:12). A debt is both a duty and something that is owed. When we owe something, it's right for us to pay. It's also a duty. Jesus says that we have a duty to love one another. Jesus says, "By this everyone will know that you are my disciples, if you love one another" (John 13:35 NIV).

Our third plea is that God "lead us not into temptation but deliver us from evil." This should not be misunderstood as God leading us into sin. James 1:13 says that "God cannot be tempted by evil, nor does he tempt anyone" (NIV).

Third in the model prayer, there is praise and commitment. The kingdom is God's, the power is God's, and the glory is God's. He has given us the kingdom and promised to transform us until this glorious kingdom fully arrives in the day of redemption.

It all belongs to God.

Surrender to God

Whenever we pray to God, we surrender to the Father.

While we can improve ourselves intellectually, physically, and in some natural things, the truth is, we cannot change our sin nature. We cannot improve ourselves without the guidance of God, and we therefore need Him if we're going to overcome in this world. The Bible says that if we're going to surrender to God, we must deny a human-centered worldview. We must deny self-sufficiency. We must deny any other god but the one True and Living God.

When we pray, we leave behind old worldviews and philosophical positions. Jesus says that we should surrender to God. He prays, "Our Father which art in heaven" (Matthew 6:9). We're not looking at the things in this world. When we surrender to heaven, it means that we look to the things that are eternal; we're not focused on the things that are temporal.

Jesus also prays, "Hallowed be thy name" (Matthew 6:9). We must approach God's name reverently.

When we come to God, bowing before Him in lowliness and humility, we recognize who we are in comparison to Him. In the light of God, we are nothing and God is everything. We come to Him humbly because we know that He is to be reverenced in every respect.

Your Kingdom Come

We must pray for God's kingdom to come (Matthew 6:10). What is God's kingdom? It is the rule and reign of God in the hearts of people.

God desires for us to perfectly submit to Him for His glory. God desires for us to be living, loving, and helping, having our being in Him and in Him alone. God wills for us to live dependent on Him instead of depending on ourselves. He wills for us to recognize and acknowledge our inadequacies.

We know Him as the Lord who provides for us. That's why we pray for His will. That's why we pray for His kingdom in a world that's filled with bitterness and evil. The kingdom of God is desperately needed. We need God's reign today. And that's what the body of Christ ought to continually pray for: "God, let Your will be done, let Your kingdom come."

We are to pray for His will to be done on the earth. Sometimes we try to negotiate His will, as though God does not know best. But whenever we pray for God's will to be done, we are praying that we would labor in a way that pleases God. We are saying that we are at His disposal for however He chooses to use us.

We must remember that God's will is never displeasing. His will is always best. Paul says in Romans 8:28, "And we know that in all things God works for the good of those who love him, who have been called according to his purpose" (NIV). Sometimes we may doubt the will of God, but we should trust God's will even when we do not completely understand it.

God's Provision

God is Jehovah-Jireh. He is the One who provides for us in abundant and bountiful ways. And because God does all those wonderful things, we must trust Him.

We should depend upon God day to day. I know the world says we have to store up for tomorrow, for the next year, and for the future. But we don't know what tomorrow holds. That's why we simply trust God to meet our needs for each day.

Forgiveness

Sometimes we are confronted with people who do things that are hurtful. I'm not saying that these things are excusable. I'm not saying that we should give license for evil to be done. But Jesus has asked us to forgive these people who hurt us.

How can you forgive somebody who hurts you? We often think that forgiveness equals forgetting what has happened to us. But when you forgive someone, you're not necessarily forgetting what they have done. What you're really doing is *choosing* not to get even with them. You're not excusing what they have done. Forgiveness means relinquishing your right to hurt them back.

We must pray that God would help us to forgive others, to give them the same grace He has given to us. Jesus said, "Blessed are the merciful: for they shall obtain mercy" (Matthew 5:7). If we can't forgive other people, we will be carrying the weight of our own guilt in our lives and we won't be set free.

You will never get even with your offender. If you try, you still won't be satisfied with the result. And the whole time you will be stuck in your own desire for revenge and you won't know God's peace. You won't know God's joy. You won't be able to move forward.

As the offended, move on and let God be God. Extend forgiveness. Demonstrate grace to the one who hurt you.

God's Protection

God may try us, prove us, and purify us. God may allow things to happen to strengthen us and teach us to endure. But God will never lead us by the awful pull of sin. Rather, we should be praying that we would not fall into temptation. There is sin lurking all around us. The enemy prowls around like a lion trying to devour, kill, steal, and destroy (1 Peter 5:8; John 10:10 NIV).

We must pray to God that He would preserve us and rescue us when we are confronted by sin. Don't be the one to fall into sin. Trust God to keep you from it. Pray for His will to be done in your life (Matthew 6:10). Pray that He will provide for you in an abundant way. Pray that you would forgive and be liberated and know His peace. Pray that you would not be led into sin but be delivered from evil (Matthew 6:13).

Give Praise to God

We ought to praise God because He is the Source of the kingdom, the power, and the glory (Matthew 6:13). God has the power to keep and preserve us. And because God can keep us, He is worthy of our praise. He is worthy of glory. He is worthy of honor.

Praise is expressing your gratitude to Him because you know that He has been good to you. It's celebrating Him because you know that without the Lord on your side, you would never have the blessings you do. It's giving God praise because you know it's Him who is keeping you. It's God who wakes you up. It's God who keeps you moving. It's God who keeps you breathing. The air that you breathe, the strength that you have—it's God who is providing for you.

He is worthy of praise. He is worthy of glory. He is worthy of honor.

Prayer Is Imperative

Prayer is a catalyst that energizes our spiritual lives. Prayer ushers us into perpetual communion with God. Prayer is the central avenue God uses to transform us. Prayer is imperative. The more we pray, the more we begin to think the thoughts of God. The more we pray, the more we begin to love the things that God loves. The more we pray, the more we begin to will the things that God wills.

As in all other areas of His life here on earth, Jesus was a model for us when He taught us to pray. Pray as He did. Pray as He taught us to pray. Pray to make a difference in your world.

LENTEN SERIES: NO GREATER LOVE:

A BIBLICAL WALK THROUGH CHRIST'S PASSION

Day and Evening classes will be offered!

Tuesday, March 12 - April 9, 10 am to 12 Noon

Saturday, March 16 - April 13, 10 am to 12 Noon

Filmed on location in the Holy Land, **No Greater Love** is a **five-part video series and full-length book** reveals Christ's amazing love for us. Best-selling author Edward Sri guides you through the last hours of Christ's life in this biblical pilgrimage. *For more information or to sign up please contact Sandy Korzick at:* stkorzick@verizon.net

...aff

410-785-0356 x716
fbrauer@archbalt.org

bsteggert@loyolablakefield.org

RLeavitt@stmarys.edu

410-785-0356 x712
deacondon@ccsfx.org

410-785-0356 x717
pallshouse@ccsfx.org

410-785-0356 x720

SACRAMENTS

Baptisms:

Baptisms are celebrated at 1:00 p.m. on the 1st Sunday of the month. You may also have your child baptized during a Mass. To schedule a Baptism or sign up for the required Baptism Prep class, please call the Parish Office and ask for Jan Kratfel, x711

WORKBOOK

Chapter Seven Questions

Question: What are some of the ways that prayer changes us?

_____

_____

_____

_____

_____

_____

_____

_____

_____

_____

Question: According to the model prayer, what things should we pray for? What attitudes should we have in prayer?

_____

_____

_____

_____

_____

_____

_____

_____

_____

_____

Action: If you have not already, memorize the Lord's Prayer. During your devotional times, try using it as a model/springboard for structuring your prayers.

Chapter Seven Notes

CHAPTER EIGHT

Jesus Changed People's Lives

And Jesus entered and passed through Jericho. And, behold, there was a man named Zacchaeus, which was the chief among the publicans, and he was rich. And he sought to see Jesus who he was; and could not for the press, because he was little of stature. And he ran before, and climbed up into a sycomore tree to see him: for he was to pass that way.

And when Jesus came to the place, he looked up, and saw him, and said unto him, Zacchaeus, make haste, and come down; for to day I must abide at thy house. And he made haste, and came down, and received him joyfully. And when they saw it, they all murmured, saying, That he was gone to be guest with a man that is a sinner.

And Zacchaeus stood, and said unto the Lord: Behold, Lord, the half of my goods I give to the poor; and if I have taken any thing from any man by false accusation, I restore him fourfold.

And Jesus said unto him, This day is salvation come to this house, forsomuch as he also is a son of Abraham. For the Son of man is come to seek and to save that which was lost.

—Luke 19:1–10

The man had messed up terribly. He had been dishonest and unjust. He had stolen from others. He had been a betrayer. He had done the unimaginable to his own people. Do you know someone like him? Perhaps the someone you know is yourself? Jesus didn't look at this man in the light of the wrong he had done. Jesus looked at the man and saw the good in him. And Jesus called that man to follow His ways of love and compassion.

He called the man named Zacchaeus.

Chief Tax Collector

Zacchaeus's story should stir hope in every person's heart, because it shows that God can convert anyone who would surrender their life to Him.

Zacchaeus represents both extremes. In one sense, he can be considered deplorable—a cheat, an unjust and dishonest man. On the other hand, he could be considered prestigious because he was a wealthy man. Everything we claim would bring us happiness—Zacchaeus had it. Yet he was still greatly troubled.

Jesus saw Zacchaeus—the *chief* among the publicans (Luke 19:2). Take note of that description. It is the only place in Scripture in which this distinction is made. The publican in the temple with the Pharisee was referred to as a tax collector. Matthew, whom Jesus called to be one of His apostles, was also a tax collector.

But in this text, it's different. Zacchaeus was a *chief* tax collector. And while the Scriptures do not completely divulge the meaning of that title, we can infer that Zacchaeus was probably the head tax collector.

Zacchaeus Desperately Sought Jesus

Although it appeared on the surface that Zacchaeus had everything together, he was empty and lonely inside, and this drove him to desperately seek Jesus. Whenever there is true conversion, it includes a desperation to seek Jesus at any cost.

Verses 3 and 4 tell us: "And he sought to see Jesus who he was; and could not for the press, because he was little of stature. And he ran before, and climbed up into a sycamore tree to see him: for he was to pass that way" (Luke 19:3–4).

Zacchaeus was a Jew who worked for the Roman government. The Roman government allowed tax collectors to charge the taxpayers more than the required amount of taxes and keep the rest of the money for themselves. Zacchaeus would therefore charge in excess and pocket the extra money. In many instances, tax collectors would take bribes from the rich who wanted to avoid taxes. In other cases, they would seek to swindle the average citizen.

Zacchaeus charged his own people taxes. Because he was an unjust cheat, the Jews had ostracized him; he had betrayed his own nation and denied his Jewish heritage. This helps to explain why he was so lonely.

Zacchaeus shows us that it's not about the things we possess. He was empty and lonely because he was despised. And yet he was also humble. He was so desperate to see Jesus, he wouldn't let anything stop him. He had the audacity to try to see Jesus despite the press all around Him. Here was a man of prestige, a man of power. And he humbled himself to the point that he actually climbed a tree. Can you imagine a person with such dignity and position—*climbing a tree?*

It might have even been dangerous for him to go out among the people who hated him so much. He might have gotten beaten up. Can you imagine how he could have been abused? Can you imagine the number of people who wanted to get even with Zacchaeus? And yet he had the boldness to go right through the crowds. The Bible says he even ran before the crowds and then he climbed up a tree. It wasn't just seeing Jesus physically that Zacchaeus was after. It was experiencing Jesus.

Zacchaeus demonstrated his persistence and determination despite the threat the mob may have presented for him.

Zacchaeus Received Jesus' Invitation

The Bible says in verse 5, "And when Jesus came to the place, he looked up, and saw him, and said unto him, Zacchaeus, make haste, and come down; for to day I must abide at thy house. And he made haste" (Luke 19:5–6). That was his response—he came down and received Him joyfully.

Just as Jesus looked up and saw Zacchaeus in the tree, God sees us no matter where we are. God sees the person who's seeking Him. He knows our need and reaches out to meet that need.

Zacchaeus was in the right place. He was determined to take whatever steps were necessary to see Jesus. He put himself in the right place—in a position of humility. And Jesus not only saw him, but He called Zacchaeus by name, which must have shocked him.

True Conversion

Zacchaeus came down, and the Bible says he repented. The evidence of Zacchaeus's authentic repentance is seen in his changed behavior:

> *And he made haste, and came down, and received him joyfully. And when they saw it, they all murmured, saying, That he was gone to be guest with a man that is a sinner.*

> *And Zacchaeus stood, and said unto the Lord: Behold, Lord, the half of my goods I give to the poor; and if I have taken any thing from any man by false accusation, I restore him fourfold.*
>
> *—Luke 19:6–8*

We can understand repentance through magnetism—the exertion of electrons. The motion of atoms within an electron determines the gravitational pull, or the attraction. We were born into sin, and so it's easy for us to gravitate toward sin. You put two magnets on the table, and if they're facing each other, a gravitational pull will cause them to try to connect with each other.

But when you repent, it's as if you go from an attraction to a repulsion, just as magnets will repel each other if you turn them in the opposite direction.

Zacchaeus had stolen from, cheated, and betrayed his own. But then he told Jesus, "All the good that I have, fifty percent of it I'm giving back. Whatever I have accumulated for myself, I'm giving fifty percent of it back. I'm also giving back to those from whom I stole—fourfold" (see Luke 19:8).

The Mosaic Law said if a person was going to make things right through restitution, at least twofold repayment was required (Exodus 22:4). But Zacchaeus said he was giving back *fourfold*. And Jesus said to him, "This day is salvation come to this house, forsomuch as he also is a son of Abraham" (Luke 19:9). Because Zacchaeus had the faith of Abraham, not only did salvation come to him that day, but it also came to his house.

Seek Jesus Desperately

Are you so passionate to seek Jesus that you are unconcerned about the estimations and the opinions of other people around you?

In a world that pays no attention to Jesus, we must be a people who pursue Him wholeheartedly. We must not pursue Him halfway; we must run all the way to Jesus.

People may not like me. They may talk about me and seek to belittle me. But come what may, I will pursue the heart of Jesus.

When you're desperate for Jesus, it doesn't matter what others think. When you really want Jesus, nothing can stop you. It's faith that drives you to pursue Jesus at any cost.

Independent of Him, we're just thoughtlessly meandering along, trying to figure out life. But when He takes up residence in our hearts, we are really living.

Zacchaeus had a faith that moved him closer to Jesus. Perhaps he heard the report that Jesus had once saved another tax collector by the name of Matthew and brought him into His inner circle. And if Jesus did that for Matthew—another publican or tax collector— Zacchaeus likely believed He could do it for him. He must have thought, *This Messiah I've heard about, this One who came to bring hope and peace and life, surely He can take my messed-up life, my sins, my mistakes, and my broken pieces, and restore me to newness of life.*

When people call us by name, there is a natural tendency for our ears to perk up and our senses to become more alert. Jesus knows your name! When He calls you, He calls you by name.

But we must respond as Zacchaeus did. We must stay in the place where Jesus will see us. We need to stop hiding behind the crowd. We must stop hiding behind our past. And we must stop hiding behind our mistakes. We must come to Jesus just as we are.

God has called us to move forward. And we need to do it with haste. I may not be getting there as fast as the next person, but at least I'm headed to where I'm going. And as long as we're moving forward, God can use us.

When you really repent, it will change the way you do things, your values, your priorities. It will change your life. Zacchaeus turned his life around and surrendered to God and His righteousness. The crowd looked at Jesus and said, "How dare He eat with a confessed and known sinner?" (Luke 19:7).

Zacchaeus gave up everything so that not only he but his whole household could be saved. Repentance changed his life. When you really change, you won't worry about the people who criticize you.

We all need Jesus. Like Zacchaeus, no matter how prestigious or deplorable we may seem to others, we need Jesus. Jesus sees you. He's calling your name. Do whatever it takes to respond to Him.

WORKBOOK

Chapter Eight Questions

Question: What was Zacchaeus's role and how did it relate to his standing in the community? What kind of position would you compare this to today?

_____

_____

_____

_____

_____

_____

_____

_____

_____

_____

_____

_____

Question: What does it look like to pursue Jesus whole-heartedly?

_____

_____

_____

_____

_____

_____

_____

_____

_____

_____

Action: Zacchaeus demonstrated his repentance through his actions. What concrete step can you take to show that Jesus has truly changed your life? What is something the "old you" would never have done that the "redeemed you" can now do through Christ?

Chapter Eight Notes

_____

_____

_____

_____

_____

_____

_____

_____

_____

_____

_____

_____

_____

_____

_____

_____

_____

_____

CHAPTER NINE

Jesus Is the Christ

When Jesus came into the coasts of Caesarea Philippi, he asked his disciples, saying, Whom do men say that I the Son of man am? And they said, Some say that thou art John the Baptist: some, Elias; and others, Jeremias, or one of the prophets.

He saith unto them, But whom say ye that I am? And Simon Peter answered and said, Thou art the Christ, the Son of the living God.

And Jesus answered and said unto him, Blessed art thou, Simon Barjona: for flesh and blood hath not revealed it unto thee, but my Father which is in heaven. And I say also unto thee, That thou art Peter, and upon this rock I will build my church; and the gates of hell shall not prevail against it. And I will give unto thee the keys of the kingdom of heaven: and whatsoever thou shalt bind on earth shall be bound in heaven: and whatsoever thou shalt loose on earth shall be loosed in heaven. Then charged he his disciples that they should tell no man that he was Jesus the Christ.

—Matthew 16:13–20

Who Is Jesus?

Who is Jesus?

That question has been asked by countless people since the time of His ministry. Some people asked Him the question directly on occasion—but sometimes, He asked *them*!

Jesus and His disciples had journeyed from the Sea of Galilee to Caesarea Philippi near Mount Hermon. There, Jesus had an intimate discussion with His disciples.

He was approaching the culmination of His earthly ministry. The end was coming soon, and it was imperative for Him to reveal to them who He really was.

There is only one answer to this question: "Thou art the Christ, the Son of the Living God" (Matthew 16:16).

Caesarea was known as a religious place, filled with the worship of all kinds of gods. It was against this dramatic backdrop that Jesus presented this question to His disciples, asking them, "Whom do men say that I the Son of man am?" (Matthew 16:13).

Peter's Confession

The disciples began to answer from different perspectives: "Some say that thou art John the Baptist" (Matthew 16:14).

The common people saw the similarities between John and Jesus. They both did great work. They both performed miracles. They were both divinely chosen by God and gifted by God. They both proclaimed the kingdom of God and prophesied that people should be ready for the kingdom of God. So, many people looked at John and Jesus and thought that they were on the same mission.

Others called Him Elijah (Matthew 16:14). Malachi 4:5 had said that Elijah would come before the Messiah. Some said, "Thou art Jeremiah" (Matthew 16:14). Jeremiah had revealed great things about God and religion. Many believed that Jeremiah would return, bringing with him the tabernacle, the altar, and the ark of the covenant.

Some said, "Thou art a prophet" (Matthew 16:14). Perhaps Jesus was just another prophet who had come to give them a great new philosophy about life.

But Jesus didn't come to proclaim the significance of who God is. He is the Messiah. He is our Redeemer. He is the One who sacrificed His own life so that we might have life.

In verse 15, Jesus asked, "But whom say ye that I am?" (Matthew 16:15). And it's more emphatic in the Greek, because He looked at them and said, "But *you*, who do *you* say that I am?" (Matthew 16:15).

Peter answered, "Thou art the Christ, the Son of the living God" (Matthew 16:16). Here was a simple yet profound confession arising from a heart of conviction.

It's the kind of confession that saves the soul of men. It's the kind of confession that lays the foundation of the Church—that Jesus Christ is the Lord.

Peter essentially declared, "I know You are the Messiah. I know You are the Son of God. I know You are the Christ. I know You were sent to fulfill the prophecies of old. I know You are the Anointed One, the One who was sent."

Peter could not have made this confession had it not been for the Lord Himself. As Jesus said, "Flesh and blood did not reveal this to you" (Matthew 16:17 NASB). This confession is revealed by God alone. Man is flesh and blood. We may have good intentions, but no man can lead another man to the conviction that leads to a regenerating power.

The work is done only by God. He uses us as His instruments, His servants, His vessels, to proclaim His Word. But the salvation is of Him. Paul declared, "For by grace are ye saved through faith; and that not of yourselves: it is the gift of God: Not of works, lest any man should boast" (Ephesians 2:8–9).

According to 1 Corinthians 2:14, the natural man cannot receive the things that are spiritual. Man understands what is earthly. But Jesus is of God and the heavens, and God revealed this to Peter.

And just like Peter, for us to understand the things that are spiritual, we must be reborn. If we're going to come to God, we need the Word of God. We need Christ, the all-sufficient One.

This confession is the foundation of the Church: "And I say also unto thee, That thou art Peter, and upon this rock I will build my church; and the gates of hell shall not prevail against it" (Matthew 16:18).

Christ said that He would build His Church, and the gates of hell would not prevail against it (Matthew 16:18). Christ is the One who oversees His Church. He is the chief cornerstone (Ephesians 2:20 NIV). The Shepherd is the leader of the sheep (John 10:11).

Who Is Jesus to You?

Jesus said, "I am the way, the truth, and the life: no man cometh unto the Father, but by me" (John 14:6). Until we look to Jesus and Him alone, we will be on a long journey, always coming up empty-handed. Keep looking to Jesus, the Author and the Finisher of your faith (Hebrews 12:2). He has given you new life (Romans 6:4 NIV), and by His Spirit, He is working things out for your good (Romans 8:28 NIV). No matter how hopeless the world may become, Jesus is still our hope.

What really matters is this question: Who is Jesus to you? It's a personal question that every individual must answer.

Even if we choose not to answer it now, the Bible says that every one of us is going to call His name someday. His name is above every name. His name is exalted above every name. Every knee shall bow, and every tongue will confess that He is Lord (Philippians 2:9–11 NIV).

You may not do it today. But your tongue will someday confess that He is Lord. I just want to encourage you: It would be good to do it voluntarily today! It's best that we recognize He is Lord now. This means that nothing else reigns in our life but the Lord Jesus Christ Himself.

We can't give ourselves spiritual life. We can't transform ourselves. We can't redeem ourselves. We can't cause ourselves to be reborn. We can't infuse eternal life within ourselves. That's why we must recognize Christ—the Son of the living God.

WORKBOOK

Chapter Nine Questions

Question: Who do the people in our world typically say
Jesus is? Who do *you* say He is?

_____

_____

_____

_____

_____

_____

_____

_____

_____

_____

Question: "Until we look to Jesus and Him alone, we will be on a long journey, always coming up empty-handed." Where are some other places, and who are some other people to whom we might look, and be left empty?

_____

_____

_____

_____

_____

_____

_____

_____

_____

_____

_____

Action: Choose an activity or a source of comfort to which you are tempted to "look" instead of to Jesus. (Examples might include music, social media, or comfort food.) Try fasting from that activity for a week or more and use your "hunger" for it as a reminder to look to Jesus.

Chapter Nine Notes

_____

_____

_____

_____

_____

_____

_____

_____

_____

_____

_____

_____

_____

_____

_____

_____

CHAPTER TEN

Jesus Went a Little Farther

Then cometh Jesus with them unto a place called Geth-semane, and saith unto the disciples, Sit ye here, while I go and pray yonder. And he took with him Peter and the two sons of Zebedee, and began to be sorrowful and very heavy. Then saith he unto them, My soul is exceeding sor-rowful, even unto death: tarry ye here, and watch with me. And he went a little farther, and fell on his face, and prayed, saying, O my Father, if it be possible, let this cup pass from me: nevertheless not as I will, but as thou wilt.

And he cometh unto the disciples, and findeth them asleep, and saith unto Peter, What, could ye not watch with me one hour? Watch and pray, that ye enter not into temptation: the spirit indeed is willing, but the flesh is weak. He went away again the second time, and prayed, saying, O my Father, if this cup may not pass away from me, except I drink it, thy will be done.

And he came and found them asleep again: for their eyes were heavy. And he left them, and went away again, and prayed the third time, saying the same words. Then cometh he to his disciples, and saith unto them, Sleep on now, and take your rest: behold, the hour is at hand, and the Son of man is betrayed into the hands of sinners. Rise, let us be going: behold, he is at hand that doth betray me.
—Matthew 26:36–46

What do you do when what you *know* you're supposed to do doesn't seem to be working?

Here is the answer: Keep on doing it. When you're struggling with doing right, it's because you're depending on your own strength. God will let you keep struggling with it until you say, "Let God." And when you let God, He will show you who's really in control. That's the message of the Garden of Gethsemane.

The Garden of Gethsemane

Jesus took His disciples along with Him to the Garden of Gethsemane. He wanted them to share in the dark hour that He was to experience.

For it was through this experience that they would observe the Savior being dependent upon God. And it would help them to overcome their own disillusionment that was yet to come.

Jesus reached the entrance of Gethsemane, sat down eight of His disciples, and then went a little farther on with Peter, James, and John.

The twelfth disciple, Judas, had already betrayed Jesus and was preparing to meet Him in the Garden of Gethsemane, where he would bring those who would put Jesus on trial, convict Him, and ultimately crucify Him.

Jesus said to Peter, James, and John, "Watch and pray with me" (Matthew 26:41). And He went yet farther into the Garden of Gethsemane to be alone with God and to pray.

Jesus was preparing to die.

The very basic definition of death is simply "separation." There are three types of death that the Bible talks about. There's physical death: the absence of life from the human body. There is spiritual death: not having a relationship with God. And there is eternal death: to die physically having never established a relationship with the Lord Jesus Christ, and to live forever separated from God.

When Jesus was in the Garden of Gethsemane, He was troubled in His human nature. He said to God, "If there be any other way let it be. But if not nevertheless thy will be done" (Matthew 26:39). His human nature surfaced in the fact that He did not want to take the cup of death.

Yet He then said, "Nevertheless, not as I will, but as You will" (Matthew 26:39).

Jesus Suffered Agonizing Grief

Jesus felt heaviness in His heart. He felt pain and overwhelming emotion deep within in Himself. He experienced incredible sorrow. Everything He had gone through and everything He was preparing to endure was there in His mind. He bore in His mind the reality of His rejection by His own people, the Jews. He contended with the malice of world leaders who were both Jews and Gentiles, religious and civic leaders. He took to heart the fact that one of His own followers, Judas, was about to betray Him. Even Peter would deny Him very soon.

His own disciples were deserting Him. Imagine the injustice of His trial that was weighing on His mind, and the ridicule and pain that Jesus was about to undergo: He would be scourged, spat upon, have a crown of thorns thrust on His head, be nailed to a cross, and be pierced in His side.

He had a mental vision that literally compressed his physical being. Jesus was so overwhelmed with sorrow that He was sweating blood. And if it had not been for God sending an angel to strengthen Him (Luke 22:43–44), it would have killed Him.

Jesus asked those in His inner circle—Peter, James, and John—to watch and pray, to partner with Him in prayer for comfort and strength. And His disciples had the audacity to fall asleep.

Watch what Jesus did in the midst of His suffering—He turned to God.

Jesus Turned to God

Verse 39 says, "He went a little farther and fell on His face, and prayed, saying, 'O My Father, if it is possible, let this cup pass from Me; nevertheless, not as I will, but as You will'" (Matthew 26:39).

In the midst of His suffering and grief, He got alone and prayed to God. He lay prostrate, His face on the ground. He cried out to God, saying, "O my Father" (Matthew 26:19). The "O" emphasized His brokenness, how He was weighed down with anguish. But He also cried, "My Father" (Matthew 26:39). This gives the picture of a little child crying out to his father in loving trust and dependency, knowing his father will hear him.

What was this cup (Matthew 26:39)? The separation. It's not to say that Jesus was fearful of death. He understood that He had come to be the Savior. Throughout His earthly ministry, He had prepared His disciples for the fact that He was going to die.

Jesus was not fearing death. He was fearing being separated from the Father.

Bearing our sin made Jesus' death different from the natural death of man. He didn't just die for one man's sin. He died for the past, the present, and the future. Jesus took all the sins of the whole world upon Himself.

His human nature did not want to be separated from the Father, but His divine nature said, "Nevertheless, if this is the only means for redemption ... if this is the only way that we will bring salvation unto a fallen humanity—let it be" (Matthew 26:39).

Jesus Stood Alone

Verse 40 and 41 say this: "Then He came to the disciples and found them sleeping, and said to Peter, "What! Could you not watch with Me one hour? Watch and pray, lest you enter into temptation. The spirit indeed is willing, but the flesh is weak" (Matthew 26:40–41).

Jesus discovered that His disciples were asleep. They were overwhelmed with mental exhaustion, physical weariness, and emotional fatigue.

God Is Present with You

Jesus wanted His disciples to understand that this was a troubling moment for Him—and for them. But the disciples refused to watch and pray. When we watch and pray, it demonstrates our reliance upon God. It demonstrates that we trust God alone. Our failure to watch and pray reveals our dependence upon our own wisdom and strength.

Jesus's friends went to sleep on Him, but He still prayed to God.

When your friends can't be there for you, you may be alone, but you don't have to be lonely because God is present with you. His promises and His power will keep and preserve you. Jesus stood alone, neglected by His friends, but God still kept Him.

That's why you don't ever stop doing what you know is right. Jesus prayed not just once, but a number of times. In fact, the Bible says He prayed three times that God would take this cup from Him (Matthew 26:44). When all hell is breaking loose in your life, just keep on praying, because God will use your Gethsemane experience to take you to a place you would have never thought possible.

Whenever you hit trouble, know God is at work. And if you go a little farther, like Jesus did, eventually you'll experience His joy.

WORKBOOK

Chapter Ten Questions

Question: What made Gethsemane so agonizing for Jesus?

Question: Describe a time when you felt abandoned or betrayed by your friends. How did you experience God's presence during that time?

_____

_____

_____

_____

_____

_____

_____

_____

_____

_____

Action: "Watch and pray." Ask God to lay a burden on your heart for what He wants you to pray about. This could be a personal situation or a burden for a friend. Then "watch and pray" for one hour as the disciples were asked to do.

Chapter Ten Notes

_____

_____

_____

_____

_____

_____

_____

_____

_____

_____

_____

_____

_____

_____

_____

_____

_____

_____

Jesus Did God's Will

And he went a little farther, and fell on his face, and prayed, saying, O my Father, if it be possible, let this cup pass from me: nevertheless not as I will, but as thou wilt.
—Matthew 26:39

Jesus was finally in the shadow of the cross. The purpose for which He had come to earth was looming before Him. But now that He finally faced His most difficult and terrible task, He had a decision to make.

Up to this point, Jesus had been tested in every respect and emerged victorious. He did not have any sin in Him (1 John 3:5). But as He prayed in the Garden, He felt the weight of the world's sin upon Him (2 Corinthians 5:21). Jesus, in His divinity, could foresee everything that awaited Him at the cross. And in His humanness, He sought a way of escape.

The question is—*was* there a way of escape? Was there another means or method to bring redemption to a fallen humanity? Jesus prayed, "O my Father, if this cup may not pass away from me, except I drink it, thy will be done" (Matthew 26:42).

The implied answer to Jesus' prayer is that our only means to redemption and reconciliation was for Jesus to go to the cross. After Jesus petitioned God, He prayed and settled in His spirit what He needed to do.

He said, "If this cup may not pass away from me, except I drink it, thy will be done" (Matthew 26:42). Jesus exemplified for us that, regardless of the sacrifices we may have to make in life, we must have the same mind as Christ: "Thy will be done" (Matthew 26:42).

God's Will for Jesus

God had mapped out the plan for Jesus' life long before He was a baby in a manger. And Jesus gave testimony to this truth.

When He was twelve years old and was left behind by his parents in Jerusalem, He was in the temple discussing religious laws with the religious leaders. When His earthly father and mother came back to find Him, He said to them, "I must be about my Father's business" (Luke 2:49).

God had a plan for Jesus and He has a will for every life, but people can pervert the purposes of God.

God is sovereign. He is omniscient, which means that He is all-knowing.

People have messed up in all kinds of circumstances. The truth of the matter is that even Jesus Himself in His humanness was tempted to diverge from God's will.

Is it possible that Jesus could have refused to go to the cross? Is it possible that Jesus could have yielded to the temptations of Satan when He was in the wilderness? In His human nature, He could have done this. But in His divine nature, He surrendered completely and wholly to God. That ought to serve as an encouragement to us.

The Savior was crucified because it was the sovereign will of God. Jesus prayed, "If this cup may not pass away from me, except I drink it, thy will be done" (Matthew 26:42).

It was the sovereign will of God to send His Son, Jesus Christ, to Calvary so that we might be redeemed.

God's Will for You

Jesus knew exactly who He was and what He was about. He knew the will of God. Just like God had a plan and purpose for His Son, He has a plan for your life. God can use you for His glory. The Bible says in Jeremiah that before you were formed in your mother's womb, God had plans for you, plans to prosper you (Jeremiah 1:5; Jeremiah 29:11 NIV). George W. Truett said that to find the will of God is the greatest discovery, and to do the will of God is the greatest achievement.[7]

God can use you, whom He loves dearly. God will use you as a vessel to display His glory. God will use you as an instrument to sound forth His truth and change this world.

When you come to Him and surrender your life, God will bless you beyond what you can imagine. When you know God's will, there is a peace beyond measure. You will find true contentment and satisfaction when you are walking in the will of God.

Sometimes God's will is not convenient. Sometimes it doesn't fit with your plans. But if you do the will of God, you will experience blessings beyond measure.

When we think about God's love and sacrifice, we ought to surrender unto Him and be willing to do His will for His glory and for our benefit.

You've got to do what God has called and gifted you to do for His glory—even when you're not applauded. God deserves this glory.

God is powerful enough to bring forth whatever it is that's consistent with His will. Yet God gave humanity free will. So, there is a chance that we might deviate from what God intends for us to do and to be.

It was essential that man was given free will, or we could never love God with sincerity. If it was not for free will, we would be mindless robots programmed to say, "I love you, I love you, I love you." So, God gave us free will so that we could love Him with liberty.

In our free will, we are capable of diverging from God's will. We must put safeguards around ourselves to protect us from the pitfall of disobedience. We need to spend time with God—praying and reading His Word. I'm not going to tell you it's easy, because it's not. There will always be temptation. But we've still got to stand and be determined that we will surrender our lives and commit to what God wills for us.

The more we do the will of God, the more joy we will have in life and the more peace we will have.

The essence of life is to let God's will be done. We are called to do this. And when we trust God, He will do exceedingly and abundantly above all that we could ask or even think (Ephesians 3:20).

WORKBOOK

Chapter Eleven Questions

Question: Think of a situation where God's will for you was much harder or different from what you imagined. What kept you obedient to His will even when it involved suffering?

_____

_____

_____

_____

_____

_____

_____

_____

_____

_____

_____

Question: Why did God create humanity with a free will? What is the danger of this freedom to you personally?

_____

_____

_____

_____

_____

_____

_____

_____

_____

_____

Action: Look up and study these verses about the will of God: Psalm 40:8; Mark 3:35; John 1:13; John 4:34; Romans 12:2; 1 Corinthians 1:1; 1 Thessalonians 4:3; 1 Peter 2:15; 1 John 2:17.

Chapter Eleven Notes

_____

_____

_____

_____

_____

_____

_____

_____

_____

_____

_____

_____

_____

_____

_____

_____

_____

_____

CHAPTER TWELVE

Jesus Died for Our Sins

For scarcely for a righteous man will one die: yet perad-
venture for a good man some would even dare to die. But
God commendeth his love toward us, in that, while we
were yet sinners, Christ died for us. Much more then, be-
ing now justified by his blood, we shall be saved from
wrath through him. For if, when we were enemies, we
were reconciled to God by the death of his Son, much
more, being reconciled, we shall be saved by his life. And
not only so, but we also joy in God through our Lord Jesus
Christ, by whom we have now received the atonement.
—Romans 5:7–11

Being saved is not enough.

Those of us who have surrendered our lives to Christ
live continuously beneath the shadow of the cross. We
must always remember the blood that redeemed us, for it
calls us to live a life of godliness. If we really want to
know everything that God has for us, we must hear the
message of the cross and come to Him. That's why He
died for us!

Christ has called us to serve unselfishly. We must join those who walked with Him on earth in testifying that He is the One who has given us the gift and the grace of faith that stirs us to believe in Him in the first place. And He is the One who sustains us in this. He is the Author and the Finisher of our faith (Hebrews 12:2). He is the One with whom we have a covenant relationship.

In a world that's lost in a maze of sin, He is the Way. In a world that's lost in deception and erroneous doctrine, He is the Truth. In a world sinking into death and destruction, He is Life. (John 14:6)

He died so that we might live.

Jesus Crucified

The crucifixion of Jesus is at the very heart of the gospel. All the prophecies of the Old Testament converged and found their fulfillment on the day when Jesus hung for six hours on the cross of Calvary.

Between the Garden of Gethsemane and 9 a.m. the next morning, Jesus was tried six times: three times before the Jewish court and three times before a Roman court. There were many injustices in these trials. Jesus' accusers even hired false witnesses to testify against Him (Matthew 26:57–61).

Jesus was treated shamefully, and yet He refused to speak on His own behalf (Matthew 26:62–63; 27:13–14). A crown of thorns was thrust upon His head (Matthew 27:29). He was spat upon (Matthew 27:30). He was nailed to a cross erected between two thieves (Matthew 27:35–38). His garments were taken from Him and gambled for at His crucifixion (Matthew 27:35). All of these events demonstrate the ridicule that accompanied Jesus' crucifixion.

Jesus's death was not like any other man's death. This event had been present in the mind of God ever since the creation of the world. Jesus had to die so that God's redemptive plan could be consummated. He had to die so that we could live.

The Reason

Many people ask the question, "Who is responsible for the death of Jesus?" Some people blame the Roman soldiers who seized Him (Matthew 26:47); Pontius Pilate, who gave the order to crucify Him (Matthew 27:22–26); the Jewish people who shouted to have Him crucified (Matthew 27:23); or maybe even Judas Iscariot, who betrayed Him to the Roman guard (Matthew 26:48). Yet these are all superficial ways of placing blame.

Before we blame anyone else, we had better take a good, hard look at ourselves. Each of us needs to understand that it was *our own sins* that nailed Him to the cross. Each of us has fallen short of His glory; each of us was shaped in iniquity, born into sin. He died for each of us. *We're* the reason for the crucifixion.

However, Jesus wasn't forced to die. He willingly gave His life. He said, "No one takes [my life] from me, but I lay it down of my own accord" (John 10:18 NIV). Thanks be to God that He made us, He redeemed us, and He willingly gave His life to deliver us from sin!

Yet even amid this deplorable act, God was at work. What Satan intended to use to eliminate Jesus of Nazareth—this was the one act God used to redeem a fallen humanity!

Mercy at the Cross

When we look at the cross, we can see the heart of God better than any other place in the entire Bible. He gave His only Begotten Son to die for us (John 3:16).

Jesus came to pour out His life for our sins—nobody took His life from Him (Mark 10:45). He poured out His life by His own volition (John 10:18). He told Peter in the Garden of Gethsemane, "If I wanted to pray to the Father He can send thousands of angels to rescue me, but I'm laying down my own life" (Matthew 26:53–56).

Jesus didn't lay down His life because we were deserving of this act. It was because of His mercy.

One thing I've learned is that a lost person doesn't need justice. If God dealt with all of us in terms of justice, our situation would be completely hopeless. God deals with us in mercy.

He has withheld from us what our sin warranted and has given us what we did not deserve. That's what I love about the mercy of God.

And, praise be to God, it's His mercy that's keeping us now!

The Message of the Cross

I lack the intellectual capacity, and the English language may lack the vocabulary, to expound adequately upon the full depths of the cross.

To the person who has never repented of sin or trusted Jesus Christ as Lord and Savior, the message is *come to Christ.* Confess and repent of your sins and trust the Lord Jesus Christ as your Savior. God placed all the sins for all eternity on the back of His Son.

This is what we must do if we're ever going to experience all that God desires to give to us. We must be born again. We must receive justification—the forgiveness of our sins that counts us as righteous—awarded to us at Calvary. *Justification* changes our standing before God, but *regeneration* changes our nature by the power of God and His Spirit. Regeneration is what enables us to live like Jesus. If you have never accepted Him as your Lord and Savior, the cross beckons you to come to Him today.

WORKBOOK

Chapter Twelve Questions

Question: What is the true reason for Jesus' death? Was Jesus a victim? Why or why not?

_____

_____

_____

_____

_____

_____

_____

_____

_____

_____

_____

Question: What response does the cross demand from every person?

_____

_____

_____

_____

_____

_____

_____

_____

_____

_____

_____

Action: How has the cross changed your life? Share your testimony this week. If you have yet to receive the gospel message, will today be the day you trust Jesus as your Savior?

Chapter Twelve Notes

CHAPTER THIRTEEN

Jesus Lives—and Is Coming Back!

Now upon the first day of the week, very early in the morning, they came unto the sepulchre, bringing the spices which they had prepared, and certain others with them. And they found the stone rolled away from the sepulchre. And they entered in, and found not the body of the Lord Jesus.

And it came to pass, as they were much perplexed thereabout, behold, two men stood by them in shining garments: And as they were afraid, and bowed down their faces to the earth, they said unto them, Why seek ye the living among the dead? He is not here, but is risen: remember how he spake unto you when he was yet in Galilee, Saying, The Son of man must be delivered into the hands of sinful men, and be crucified, and the third day rise again.

And they remembered his words, And returned from the sepulchre, and told all these things unto the eleven, and to all the rest. It was Mary Magdalene and Joanna, and Mary the mother of James, and other women that were with them, which told these things unto the apostles. And their words seemed to them as idle tales, and they believed them not. Then arose Peter, and ran unto the sepulchre; and stooping down, he beheld the linen clothes laid by

themselves, and departed, wondering in himself at that
which was come to pass.

—Luke 24:1–12

Is there any more powerful message than the empty
tomb? Can there be a greater demonstration of love in
human history?

The Resurrection

Some people think that the grave was opened so that
Jesus could exit, but He was actually resurrected in a
glorified body. That means there was a spiritual dimension to His glorified body, which is not hampered by
physical limitations. The opening of the grave was not
for the benefit of the Savior. It was so that the witnesses
could come in and observe the truth.

Mary Magdalene and Mary were perplexed. They
came to the grave looking for the Savior, but He wasn't
there. The angels had to remind them, "He is not here,
but He has risen. Remember how He spoke to you while
He was still in Galilee, saying that the Son of Man must
be delivered into the hands of sinful men, and be crucified, and the third day rise again" (Luke 24:6–7 NASB).

Then they remembered His words, and they ran back
to tell the apostles of the resurrected Savior. The apostles
were in Jerusalem, fearing for their lives, gripped with
doubt and skepticism.

It was Mary Magdalene, Joanna, Mary the mother of
James, and other women who told these things to the
apostles.

"And their words seemed to them as idle tales, and they believed them not" (Luke 24:11). Even the apostles did not believe what the women were telling them.

Still, they were worried and ran to the grave to see about Jesus. Peter and the other disciples thought somebody had stolen Jesus' body.

The Glorious Message of the Resurrection

The crucifixion brought about expiation—the removal of our sin. The death of Jesus brought propitiation—the removal of God's wrath. On the cross, Jesus' body was suspended between heaven and earth, bridging the gap between God and man.

His death brought reconciliation. He removed our sin, satisfied God's wrath, and then brought God and man back together. But it didn't stop there. The kingdom of darkness was torn down because we were delivered out of darkness into His marvelous light (2 Peter 2:9).

But Sunday was a day of vindication. Early Sunday morning, Jesus got up with all power in His hand. It was the day of our assurance.

Whenever defeat seems to confront you, remember His Word. Remember God's promises in your life. He lives. The resurrection serves as the crowning apologetic of Christianity. Without the resurrection, there would *be* no Christianity.

The resurrection is the foundation upon which our faith is established. If there were no resurrection, there could be no Savior, and there could be no salvation.

There could be no gift of forgiveness of sin. Nor could there be the hope of eternal life.

Believing in the resurrection of Jesus Christ is essential for us. Paul declares in Romans 10:9–10, "...if you confess with your mouth the Lord Jesus and believe in your heart that God has raised Him from the dead, you will be saved. For with the heart one believes unto righteousness, and with the mouth confession is made unto salvation" (NKJV).

Our belief in the resurrection of Jesus Christ is essential to our salvation. The resurrection is the heart of the gospel. A dead man can't save anybody. If Jesus was dead, Satan would have won the battle. Death would have had the victory, and you and I would never experience the hope of eternal life. Our faith is only as good as the person in whom we put our faith. If Jesus couldn't raise Himself from the dead, then our faith would be in vain.

Sunday morning's resurrection assured us of forgiveness of sin. Sunday morning assured us of eternal life. And because He lives, we have hope!

Christ Is Coming Again

And when he had spoken these things, while they beheld, he was taken up; and a cloud received him out of their sight. And while they looked stedfastly toward heaven as he went up, behold, two men stood by them in white apparel; Which also said, Ye men of Galilee, why stand ye gazing up into heaven? this same Jesus, which is taken up from you into heaven, shall so come in like manner as ye have seen him go into heaven.

—Acts 1:9–11

Our Hope

What great inspiration and hope we have, to know that no matter what we contend with in life, our Savior is coming back and we will live forever in His presence. We can rejoice in the fact that we have the promise of our Savior's return. The King is coming!

> *This same Jesus, which is taken up from you into heaven, shall so come in like manner as ye have seen him go into heaven.*
>
> *—Acts 1:11*

On many occasions, Jesus discouraged the disciples from expecting a temporal kingdom. Yet the idea was so deeply ingrained in their thinking that they could not forget it. Forty days after Jesus' resurrection, the disciples were still asking about it.

"Jesus, will God establish the Jewish monarchy?" Jesus gave them a mild reprimand: "It is not for you to worry" (Acts 1:6–7).

The task of the believer is to be a witness. The knowledge of the future is reserved for God.

The disciples, like every believer today, had been promised the presence of the Holy Spirit. Jesus said:

> *But you shall receive power when the Holy Spirit has come upon you; and you shall be witnesses to Me in Jerusalem, and in all Judea and Samaria, and to the end of the earth.*
>
> *—Acts 1:8 (NKJV)*

In other words, we must start where we are and trust God to take our influence and carry us where He wills.

Be faithful where you are. He promised that if you would be faithful with just a few things, He would make you a ruler over many.

God has called us to a work. God has destined us to do something. And God has provided everything that we need to be successful in doing it. God doesn't assess us as small or great—God looks at our faithfulness. All we must do is be faithful to Him.

Do what God has called you to do with what God has given you, and you will make an incredible difference in this world.

His Return Foretold

How do we really know that Christ is coming back? Some people think that Jesus coming back is merely idle speculation. But His divinely inspired Word specifically tells us that He will return.

And then shall appear the sign of the Son of man in heaven: and then shall all the tribes of the earth mourn, and they shall see the Son of man coming in the clouds of heaven with power and great glory.
—Matthew 24:30

And there shall be signs in the sun, and in the moon, and in the stars; and upon the earth distress of nations, with perplexity; the sea and the waves roaring; Men's hearts failing them for fear, and for looking after those things which are coming on the earth: for the powers of heaven

NO GREATER LOVE · 151

shall be shaken. And then shall they see the Son of man coming in a cloud with power and great glory.
                                        —Luke 21:25-27

And to wait for his Son from heaven, whom he raised from the dead, even Jesus, which delivered us from the wrath to come.
                                        —1 Thessalonians 1:10

So Christ was once offered to bear the sins of many; and unto them that look for him shall he appear the second time without sin unto salvation.
                                        —Hebrews 9:28

But the day of the Lord will come as a thief in the night...
                                        —2 Peter 3:10

But what is the point? What are God's purposes in the return of Christ to the earth?

First, Christ is coming to reveal His glory.

When He was on the earth, Jesus limited His divine glory because He wanted to identify with fallen humanity—to endure the pain, struggles, and conditions that we endure, to be confronted with the same temptations, yet to be without sin.

But when He comes the second time, every eye will see the fullness of His glory and His majesty. There won't be any holding back. We will see Him for who He is—in all of His power and glory, without any limitations.

Second, He's coming back to receive the saints: all those who express personal faith in Him, all of us who trust in Him as our Lord and Savior. We will all be caught up in the clouds to be with Him forever. The Bible promises that even those who are in the grave will be awakened and caught up with Him in the air (1 Thessalonians 4:16–17).

Finally, He's coming back to judge unbelievers (Matthew 25:41).

At this point, some people say, "That's what I have a problem with in the Church—because that seems like a God who is mean."

But it was God who gave His Son to die for me even though I was the one who sinned. He wasn't obligated to do that for me. God, by His own doing, gave His Son to die for each of us. All we have to do is surrender to Him. We don't even have to work at our salvation. We don't have to earn it. He offers it as a free gift (Ephesians 2:8). The Bible says that He gave His Son, Jesus the Christ, as a ransom for many (Matthew 20:28). And the "many" here is all-inclusive. The "many" includes people from every nation, tribe, and tongue. It doesn't matter who you are or where you've been. The "many" is all of us. The atonement is sufficient. But it's only sufficient for believers.

The only thing that could ever stop us from benefiting from what God offers through His Son is our own unbelief!

Christ's Return Is Near

There are many schools of thought about the events surrounding the coming of Christ, and it would be virtually impossible to summarize those thoughts in just one chapter. But if there is one thing that is closely associated with His coming, it is a time when Israel returns to their homeland and becomes a nation.

We also need to take into account the moral condition of this world. We live in a time when sin is no longer called sin but is considered socially acceptable. According to God's truth, however, sin is still sin and God is still displeased with it.

We are living in a time the likes of which we have hardly ever seen before. We are confronted with moral degradation and excessive immorality, and we also see a great turning away from God—a turning away from sound doctrine. People have itching ears for clever thoughts that only entertain and do not spiritually transform (2 Timothy 4:3).

There is a nearness to His coming. I can't tell you which day; I can't tell you which hour; but I can say that His coming is soon.

Prepare for Christ's Return

What can we do to prepare for Christ's coming?

The only way to truly be ready is to be saved; you must be born again. It doesn't matter how much education you have, how much money you have in your bank account, or how good-looking you are. If you do not have Jesus Christ in your heart and your life, you are eternally lost. You must repent of your sins. You must trust Jesus Christ. You must surrender your life to Him.

While we wait on His return, we must not grow complacent; we must continue to work for Him.

Jesus said, "...the Holy Ghost is come upon you: and ye shall be witnesses unto me both in Jerusalem, and in all Judaea, and in Samaria, and unto the uttermost part of the earth" (Acts 1:8). We must witness, not just with the declaration of our mouth, but also with the demonstration of our lives.

He's coming back again, whether we believe it or not.

It's been the "last days" ever since Jesus's first coming to this earth. The only reason we have not yet seen His second coming is that God is being patient with humanity and waiting for as many as possible to receive the gracious gift He offers in His Son (2 Peter 3:9).

Don't make the mistake of becoming relaxed and complacent. We must work while it is yet day, because when night comes, no man can work (John 9:4).

We must continue to work to improve ourselves and this world the best that we can by the leadership of the Holy Spirit in our daily living, but the permanent hope of our world comes through God's intervention alone. It will not always be easy, and there will be times when we may feel like giving up. That is when, more than ever, we need to endure and press into Christ for His strength.

It reminds me of when I played football. There were times when we struggled in a game and it seemed as if we were going to lose. We were beat-up, sweating, and exhausted. Every time we glanced at the scoreboard, we became even more miserable. But despite all the pain we endured during the game, if we won the victory, we forgot about the struggle and celebrated like you can't even imagine!

Listen, you may be worn out in this life that you are living for Christ. You may even think it's completely hopeless. But the King is coming! And when the King comes, we will have the victory. It is guaranteed. And when that victory comes, all the struggles of this life will be worth it.

Let us have the courage to keep fighting the good fight of faith until the day of the Lord Jesus Christ (1 Timothy 6:12).

WORKBOOK

Chapter Thirteen Questions

Question: Why was Jesus' tomb opened? What does the resurrection mean for us as believers?

_____

_____

_____

_____

_____

_____

_____

_____

_____

_____

_____

Question: "The task of the believer is to be a witness. The future is reserved for God." How did these words apply to the disciples? How do they apply to believers today?

_____

_____

_____

_____

_____

_____

_____

_____

_____

Question: What are some indicators that the return of Christ is imminent?

_____

_____

_____

_____

_____

_____

_____

_____

_____

_____

_____

Action: In light of Christ's certain return, how should we live? Write out a list of related words, such as *endure* and *watch*. Consider posting these in a place where you will see them often and be reminded of His return.

Chapter Thirteen Notes

_____

_____

_____

_____

_____

_____

_____

_____

_____

_____

_____

_____

_____

_____

_____

_____

_____

_____

_____

CONCLUSION

Follow in His Steps

To this you were called, because Christ suffered for you, leaving you an example, that you should follow in his steps.

—1 Peter 2:21 *(NIV)*

What an amazing, wonderful, unconditional love God has for us all!

God did not spare His Son but gave Him up willingly for our sake (Romans 8:32). The Son, Jesus, laid down His life (John 10:15) because of how intensely God loves us (John 3:16).

Friends, if you want to know the unconditional love of God, all you have to do is believe on the Lord Jesus Christ and accept the finished work He did on the cross and from the empty tomb (Acts 2:21).

And, fellow believers, our role now is to know Him personally, to follow the Father as the Son followed the Father, to be filled with His Spirit, and to be His witnesses in Jerusalem, Judea, Samaria, and to the ends of the earth (Acts 1:8).

We know how to do this. It's not a mystery anymore. We don't have to wander through this earthly realm, wondering why we're here. There's no need to worry if anybody loves us as we are, nor need we be confused about what we're supposed to do with our lives. We need not fret about what God's will is and whether we have the strength to live it out.

We have the example of our Lord Jesus, the Christ! He shows us everything we need to know to live the lives God has intended for us to live. Jesus has showed us the way to the Father. He showed us this in every aspect of His life. His birth; His baptism; His ministry of preaching, teaching, and healing; His love for all He met; His calling; His commissioning; His death; and His resurrection—*every* aspect of His life is our example.

He shows us how to love, how to show compassion, how to obey the Father's will, and how to persevere to the end.

Do you want to know your heavenly Father? Follow Jesus. He will lead you to Him.

Do you want to know God's will? Follow Jesus. His Spirit will reveal everything you need to know (1 John 2:27).

Do you want the strength to obey God's will? Follow Jesus. He will fill you with all strength and power (Ephesians 1:19).

Do you want to love others the way God the Father loves the whole world? Follow Jesus and His example of selfless, compassionate, sacrificial love (1 Peter 2:21).

The life of Jesus is your guide. Believe in Him, know Him, and follow Him, and you will be amazed at the blessing your life will become to you—and to everyone you meet.

REFERENCES

Notes

1. Petersen, J. Allan. "Wife Who Wanted a Divorce." *Bible.org.* https://bible.org/illustration/wife-who-wanted-divorce.
2. "Redemption." *Sermon Illustrations.* Sermons.com. http://www.sermonillustrations.com/a-z/r/redemption.htm.
3. Hendricks, Howard. *Heaven Help the Home.* Victor Books, 1990. In *Illustrations Unlimited,* edited by James S. Hewett, Tyndale House Publishers, Inc., 1998, p. 191.
4. Strong, James. "Baptizo." *Strong's Exhaustive Concordance.* In *Blue Letter Bible.* https://www.blueletterbible.org/lang/lexicon/lexicon.cfm?Strongs=G907&t=NIV.
5. "Hatred Between Jews and Samaritans." *The Word in Life Study Bible* (New Testament Edition). Thomas Nelson Publishers, 1993, p. 340–341. In *Bible.org.* https://bible.org/illustration/hatred-between-jews-and-samaritans.

6. Hillin, Taryn. "16 Ways Maya Angelou Taught Us How to Love." *The Huffington Post.* May 29, 2014. https://www.huffingtonpost.com/2014/05/28/maya-angelou-love_n_5405609.html.
7. Afolaranmi, Adebayo. *Spiritual Digest for Each Day of the Year.* Lulu.com, 2012, p. 130.

About the Author

Pastor Mouton is a native of New Iberia, Louisiana. He is married to Reba Mouton, and they are the parents of two children, Hanna and Joshuah. He is licensed and ordained and has been in ministry for more than fifteen years. Pastor Mouton holds a bachelor's in theology and a master's in Christian Education from Southwestern Baptist Theological Seminary in Fort Worth, Texas. He serves as the pastor of New Hope Missionary Baptist Church of Tampa, Florida.

About Sermon To Book

SermonToBook.com began with a simple belief: that sermons should be touching lives, *not* collecting dust. That's why we turn sermons into high-quality books that are accessible to people all over the globe.

Turning your sermon series into a book exposes more people to God's Word, better equips you for counseling, accelerates future sermon prep, adds credibility to your ministry, and even helps make ends meet during tight times.

John 21:25 tells us that the world itself couldn't contain the books that would be written about the work of Jesus Christ. Our mission is to try anyway. Because in heaven, there will no longer be a need for sermons or books. Our time is now.

If God so leads you, we'd love to work with you on your sermon or sermon series.

Visit www.sermontobook.com to learn more.

Made in the USA
Middletown, DE
03 March 2019